Every child matters

Presented to Parliament by
the Chief Secretary to the Treasury
by Command of Her Majesty
September 2003

Cm 5860   £22.00

contents

Foreword by the Prime Minister

For most parents, our children are everything to us: our hopes, our ambitions, our future. Our children are cherished and loved.

But sadly, some children are not so fortunate. Some children's lives are different. Dreadfully different. Instead of the joy, warmth and security of normal family life, these children's lives are filled with risk, fear, and danger: and from what most of us would regard as the worst possible source – from the people closest to them.

Victoria Climbié was one of those children. At the hands of those entrusted with her care she suffered appallingly and eventually died. Her case was a shocking example from a list of children terribly mistreated and abused. The names of the children involved, echoing down the years, are a standing shame to us all.

Every inquiry has brought forward proposals for change and improvement to the child protection system. There have been reforms. Things have got better for many. But the fact that a child like Victoria Climbié can still suffer almost unimaginable cruelty to the point of eventually losing her young life shows that things are still very far from right. More can and must be done.

Responding to the inquiry headed by Lord Laming into Victoria's death, we are proposing here a range of measures to reform and improve children's care – crucially, for the first time ever requiring local authorities to bring together in one place under one person services for children, and at the same time suggesting real changes in the way those we ask to do this work carry out their tasks on our and our children's behalf.

For children for whom action by the authorities has reduced the risk they face, we want to go further: we want to maximise the opportunities open to them – to improve their life chances, to change the odds in their favour. So in addition, this Green Paper puts forward ideas on a number of related issues, including parenting, fostering, young people's activities and youth justice. All these proposals are important to children's health and security.

Sadly, nothing can ever absolutely guarantee that no child will ever be at risk again from abuse and violence from within their own family. But we all desperately want to see people, practices and policies in place to make sure that the risk is as small as is humanly possible. I believe that the proposals we are putting forward here constitute a significant step towards that goal.

Tony Blair

Introduction by the Chief Secretary to the Treasury

I was delighted to be asked by the Prime Minister to lead the development of this Green Paper. Over the past year, I have met and worked with a range of practitioners, academics, policymakers and children and young people. Their influence has shaped the paper – their ideas and advice have been invaluable.

Every Child Matters is published alongside a detailed response to Lord Laming's Report into the death of Victoria Climbié, and a report produced by the Social Exclusion Unit on raising the educational attainment of children in care. I am extremely grateful to Lord Laming and his team for all their work on the inquiry that led to his report.

This Green Paper seeks views from everyone but it is addressed in particular to those vital groups of staff and professionals who are committed to meeting children's needs. The Government recognises their dedication, the progress they have made and the lead they have given, even while asking new questions and setting new challenges.

Since 1997, we have tried to put children first. We have increased the focus on prevention through the child poverty strategy, Sure Start, and our work to raise school standards. But there is still more to do. The circumstances surrounding the tragic death of Victoria Climbié bring home only too powerfully that there is no room for complacency.

We have to do more both to protect children and ensure each child fulfils their potential. Security and opportunity must go hand in hand. Child protection must be a fundamental element across all public, private and voluntary organisations. Equally, we must be ambitious for all children, whoever they are and wherever they live.

Creating a society where children are safe and have access to opportunities requires radical reform. This Green Paper builds on existing plans to strengthen preventative services by focusing on four key themes. First, we need to increase our focus on supporting families and carers – the most critical influence on children's lives. Second, we need to ensure necessary intervention before children reach crisis point and protect children from falling through the net. Third, we need to address the underlying problems identified in the Victoria Climbié Inquiry Report – weak accountability, and poor integration. Fourth, we need to ensure that the people working with children are valued, rewarded and trained.

This is the beginning of a long journey, which will present challenges for all of us, but from which we must not flinch. We will be called upon to make common cause across professional boundaries and with reformed structures and services to create the means by which the needs, interests and welfare of children can be better protected and advanced. Underpinning this must be not just the resources but an attitude that reflects the value that our society places on children and childhood.

Children are precious. The world they must learn to inhabit is one in which they will face hazards and obstacles alongside real and growing opportunities. They are entitled not just to the sentiment of adults but a strategy that safeguards them as children and realises their potential to the very best of our ability.

Paul Boateng

Executive Summary

Past failings

1 The death of Victoria Climbié exposed shameful failings in our ability to protect the most vulnerable children. On twelve occasions, over ten months, chances to save Victoria's life were not taken. Social services, the police and the NHS failed, as Lord Laming's report into Victoria's death made clear, to do the basic things well to protect her.

2 From past inquiries into the deaths of Maria Colwell and Jasmine Beckford to recent cases such as Lauren Wright and Ainlee Walker, there are striking similarities which show some of the problems are of long standing. The common threads which led in each case to a failure to intervene early enough were poor co-ordination; a failure to share information; the absence of anyone with a strong sense of accountability; and frontline workers trying to cope with staff vacancies, poor management and a lack of effective training.

3 The most tragic manifestation of these problems is when we fail to protect children at risk of harm or neglect. But the problem of children falling through the cracks between different services goes much further. Too often children experience difficulties at home or at school, but receive too little help too late, once problems have reached crisis point.

4 As Lord Laming's recommendations made clear, child protection cannot be separated from policies to improve children's lives as a whole. We need to focus both on the universal services which every child uses, and on more targeted services for those with additional needs. The policies set out in the Green Paper are designed both to protect children and maximise their potential. It sets out a framework for services that cover children and young people from birth to 19 living in England.[i] It aims to reduce the numbers of children who experience educational failure, engage in offending or anti-social behaviour, suffer from ill health, or become teenage parents.

5 We need to ensure we properly protect children at risk within a framework of universal services which support every child to develop their full potential and which aim to prevent negative outcomes. That is why this Green Paper addresses the needs of children at risk in the context of the services we provide for all children.

Where we are now

6 Over the past few years, we have seen that progress is possible:

- in education, last year we saw our best ever results in all key stages

- there are 500,000 fewer children living in households with relative low income than in 1997

- since 1997 the reconviction rate for young offenders has reduced by 22 percent

- the Government's teenage pregnancy strategy has produced a ten percent reduction in conception rates among under 18 year olds since 1998

- many of the measures put in place now, including Sure Start and measures to tackle low income through welfare to work and tax credits, will only see their full dividends in years to come.

7 But there is still more to do. Truancy remains a persistent problem. There are still too many 16 to 18 year olds not in education or training, and the educational achievement of children in care remains far too low. On many fronts, including low income, the gap in achievement between different socio-economic classes, and the number of children who are the victims of crime, we need to do more to catch up with other countries.

8 Overall, this country is still one where life chances are unequal. This damages not only those children born into disadvantage, but our society as a whole. We all stand to share the benefits of an economy and society with less educational failure, higher skills, less crime, and better health. We all share a duty to do everything we can to ensure every child has the chance to fulfil their potential.

Where we want to get to

9 Our aim is to ensure that every child has the chance to fulfil their potential by reducing levels of educational failure, ill health, substance misuse, teenage pregnancy, abuse and neglect, crime and anti-social behaviour among children and young people.

10 When we consulted children, young people and families, they wanted the Government to set out a positive vision of the outcomes we want to achieve. The five outcomes which mattered most to children and young people were:

- **being healthy:** enjoying good physical and mental health and living a healthy lifestyle

- **staying safe:** being protected from harm and neglect

- **enjoying and achieving:** getting the most out of life and developing the skills for adulthood

- **making a positive contribution:** being involved with the community and society and not engaging in anti-social or offending behaviour

- **economic well-being:** not being prevented by economic disadvantage from achieving their full potential in life.

11 The Government has built the foundations for improving these outcomes through Sure Start, raising school standards, and progress made towards eradicating child poverty. Chapter Two sets out our plans to build on these successes through:

- creating **Sure Start Children's Centres** in each of the 20 percent most deprived neighbourhoods. These combine nursery education, family support, employment advice, childcare and health services on one site

- promoting **full service extended schools** which are open beyond school hours to provide breakfast clubs and after-school clubs and childcare, and have health and social care support services on site

- increasing the focus on activities for children out of school through the creation of a **Young People's Fund with an initial budget of £200 million**

- increasing investment in **child and adolescent mental health services (CAMHS)** to deliver a ten percent increase in CAMHS capacity each year for the next three years. All areas are expected to put in place a comprehensive CAMHS by 2006

- improving **speech and language therapy.** The forthcoming National Service Framework for Children will set out proposals to improve services, including training para-professionals, supported by specialist staff

- **tackling homelessness.** By March 2004, no homeless family with children should be placed in bed and breakfast accommodation, unless in a short term emergency

- **reforms to the youth justice system.** The Government intends to revise the Child Safety Order to make it more effective and build on the success of the Intensive Supervision and Surveillance Programme by using it more widely as an alternative to custody. We will also create a new range of community sentences and make greater use of a wider range of residential placements such as intensive fostering for young offenders, including for 10 and 11 year old persistent offenders.

Green Paper proposals

12 We are building on the progress already made by focusing action on four main areas:

- supporting parents and carers

- early intervention and effective protection

- accountability and integration – locally, regionally and nationally

- workforce reform

Supporting parents and carers

13 The Government intends to put supporting parents and carers at the heart of its approach to improving children's lives where support is needed or wanted. To build additional capacity in this area, the Government has announced the creation of a Parenting Fund of £25 million over the next three years. We are consulting on a long term vision to improve parenting and family support through:

- **universal services** such as schools, health and social services and childcare providing information and advice and engaging parents to support their child's development

- **targeted and specialist support** to parents of children requiring additional support

- **compulsory action** through Parenting Orders as a last resort where parents are condoning a child's truancy, anti-social behaviour or offending.

14 All children deserve the chance to grow up in a loving, secure family. Through the adoption modernisation programme, local authorities are already delivering significant increases in adoption of looked after children. The Adoption and Children Act 2002 will further strengthen this programme of reform. This Green Paper consults on measures to tackle the recruitment and retention challenges in foster care, and to ensure that foster carers have the skills and support they need to care for vulnerable children. The Government is seeking suggestions for radical and imaginative ways of encouraging people to become foster carers and ensuring they are valued and recognised.

Early intervention and effective protection

15 Some children will always require extra help because of the disadvantages they face. The key is to ensure children receive services at the first onset of problems, and to prevent any children slipping through the net. We will do this by:

- **improving information sharing** between agencies to ensure all local authorities have a list of children in their area, the services each child has had contact with, and the contact details of the relevant professionals who work with them. The Government will remove the legislative barriers to better information sharing, and the technical barriers to electronic information sharing through developing a single unique identity number, and common data standards on the recording of information

- **developing a common assessment framework.** We will expect every local authority to identify a lead official with responsibility for ensuring information is collected and shared across services for children, covering special educational needs, Connexions, Youth Offending Teams, health, and social services. The aim is for basic information to follow the child to reduce duplication

- **introducing a lead professional.**
  Children known to more than one specialist agency should have a single named professional to take the lead on their case and be responsible for ensuring a coherent package of services to meet the individual child's needs

- **developing on the spot service delivery.** Professionals will be encouraged to work in multi-disciplinary teams based in and around schools and Children's Centres. They will provide a rapid response to the concerns of frontline teachers, childcare workers and others in universal services.

Accountability and integration – locally, regionally and nationally

16 We want to put children at the heart of our policies, and to organise services around their needs. Radical reform is needed to break down organisational boundaries. The Government's aim is that there should be one person in charge locally and nationally with the responsibility for improving children's lives. Key services for children should be integrated within a single organisational focus at both levels. To achieve this the Government will:

- legislate to create the post of **Director of Children's Services**, accountable for local authority education and children's social services

- legislate to create **a lead council member for children**

- in the long term, integrate key services for children and young people under the Director of Children's Services as part of **Children's Trusts**. These bring together local authority education and children's social services, some children's health services, Connexions and can include other services such as Youth Offending Teams. Children's Trusts will normally be part of the local authority and will report to local elected members

- require local authorities to work closely with public, private and voluntary organisations to improve outcomes for children. Local authorities will be given flexibility over how this partnership working is undertaken

- in relation to child protection, require the creation of **Local Safeguarding Children Boards** as the statutory successors to Area Child Protection Committees.

17 To support local integration, the Government has created a new **Minister for Children, Young People and Families** in the Department for Education and Skills to co-ordinate policies across Government. The Government has brought responsibility for children's social services, family policy, teenage pregnancy, family law, and the Children and Family Court Advisory and Support Service (CAFCASS) in DfES.

18 The Government will encourage joining up locally by:

- ensuring children are a priority across services. Local bodies such as the police and health organisations will, subject to consultation, have a new duty to safeguard children, promote their well-being and work together through these partnership arrangements. We intend to give local authorities a duty to promote the educational achievement of children in care

- setting out clear practice standards expected of each agency in relation to children

- rationalising performance targets, plans, funding streams, financial accountability and indicators

- creating an integrated inspection framework for children's services. Ofsted will take the lead in bringing together joint inspection teams. This will ensure services are judged on how well they work together

- creating an improvement and intervention function to drive up performance by sharing effective practice, and intervening where services are failing.

19 Real service improvement is only attainable through involving children and young people and listening to their views. This Green Paper sets out proposals for a new **Children's Commissioner** to act as an independent champion for children,

particularly those suffering disadvantage. The Commissioner will report annually to Parliament through the Secretary of State.

Workforce reform

20 The people who work with children are central to keeping them safe and helping them get the most out of life. We owe a debt of gratitude for the difficult and challenging work that they perform. We want to value the specific skills that people from different professional backgrounds bring, and we also want to break down the professional barriers that inhibit joint working, and tackle recruitment and retention problems. Our goal must be to make working with children an attractive, high status career, and to develop a more skilled and flexible workforce. Over time, and subject to consultation and resources, the Government would like to develop a package of measures to deliver this:

- a workforce reform strategy to improve the skills and effectiveness of the children's workforce developed in partnership with local employers and staff. This will review rewards, incentives and relativities across children's practice with the aim of moving towards a framework that fairly rewards skills and responsibilities, and ensures effective incentives for good practitioners to stay on the front line

- a high profile recruitment campaign for entry into the children's workforce

- a comprehensive workload survey to address bureaucracy, and identify ways of freeing up time for face to face work with children and families

- more flexible and attractive training routes into social work, including expanding work-based training routes for graduates

- common occupational standards across children's practice linked to modular qualifications which allow workers to move between jobs more easily

- a common core of training for those who work solely with children and families and those who have wider roles (such as GPs and the police) to help secure a consistent response to children's and families' needs and a better understanding of professional roles

- a review undertaken by the Chief Nursing Officer of the contribution that health visitors and other nurses and midwives can make for children at risk

- a leadership development programme to foster high calibre leadership.

21 The development and delivery of workforce proposals will be taken forward through two new bodies. A **Children's Workforce Unit**, based in the Department for Education and Skills, will develop a pay and workforce strategy for those who work with children. The Children's Workforce Unit will work with the relevant employers, staff and Government Departments to establish a **Sector Skills Council (SSC) for Children and Young People's Services** to deliver key parts of the strategy.

Next steps

22 The Government welcomes your views on the framework set out in this consultation document. We intend to develop a strong partnership with our stakeholders – practitioners, academics, policymakers and children and young people. We would like your views on the overall vision for children's and families' services, the implementation priorities within it, and the practicalities that need to be tackled to deliver it. Subject to the outcome of this consultation, the Government intends to introduce legislation as soon as Parliamentary time allows.[ii]

---

i   The Green Paper covers all children in England. The policies and proposals it contains apply to England only except where they relate to non-devolved responsibilities, such as Home Office Services, where they apply equally to Wales. Both the Welsh Assembly Government and the Scottish Executive have expressed keen interest in and closely followed the development of the Green Paper and they will each consider which parts of the approach being adopted in England they will seek to adapt respectively.

ii A Regulatory Impact Assessment (RIA) to accompany the proposals contained in this Green Paper has been prepared and is available on the DfES website at: www.dfes.gov.uk/everychildmatters
In addition to commenting on the Green Paper proposals, you may wish to comment on the contents of the RIA, which will be revised during the course of the consultation to take account of up-to-date information.

The Challenge

This Government has invested heavily in policies designed to give all children the chance to succeed. There have already been significant improvements in educational achievement, and reductions in teenage pregnancy, re-offending and children living in low income households. Today's children and young people experience wider opportunities and benefit from rising prosperity, better health and education than those in previous generations.

However, there is still more to do. Whilst most children and young people are doing well, a significant minority experience problems that may lead to poor outcomes both during childhood and later in life. Truancy remains a persistent problem. There are too many 16 to 18 year olds not in education or training, and the educational achievement of children in care remains far too low. The tragic death of Victoria Climbié shows that some children fall through the net and are not adequately protected. We need to ensure we properly protect children at risk of neglect and harm within a framework of universal services which aims to prevent negative outcomes and support every child to develop their full potential.

This Chapter sets out:

- our goals for children and young people

- how well we are doing in relation to them

- what factors shape children's life chances

- what policy challenges need be addressed.

Our goals for children and young people

1.1 This Green Paper sets out policies to reduce the number of children who experience educational failure, suffer ill health, become pregnant as teenagers, are the victims of abuse and neglect, or become involved in offending and anti-social behaviour.

1.2 When we consulted children, young people and families they wanted the

Government to set out these aims in terms of a positive vision of what, as a society, we want to achieve for our children. They wanted an approach that was less about intervening at points of crisis or failure, and more about helping every child to achieve his or her potential. They wanted an approach that involved children, families, communities and public services working to a shared set of goals, rather than narrow or contradictory objectives.

1.3 There was broad agreement that five key outcomes really matter for children and young people's well-being:

- **being healthy:** enjoying good physical and mental health and living a healthy lifestyle

- **staying safe:** being protected from harm and neglect and growing up able to look after themselves

- **enjoying and achieving:** getting the most out of life and developing broad skills for adulthood

- **making a positive contribution:** to the community and to society and not engaging in anti-social or offending behaviour

- **economic well-being:** overcoming socio-economic disadvantages to achieve their full potential in life.

1.4 Everyone in our society has a responsibility for securing these outcomes. Families, communities, Government, public services, voluntary organisations, business, the media and others have a crucial part to play in valuing children, protecting them, promoting their interests and listening to their views.

1.5 Achieving these outcomes has benefits for children, families, and society as a whole. Children gain through improved health, well-being and prosperity now and in the future. Future generations benefit as we know that children of parents who experienced poverty, were in public care, or teenage parents are more likely to experience poor outcomes than their peers.

1.6 Society as a whole benefits through reduced spending on problems that can be avoided and through maximising the contribution to society of all citizens. For instance, a child with a conduct disorder at age 10 will cost the public purse around £70,000 by age 28 – up to ten times more than a child with no behavioural problems.[i] The overall cost of providing foster and residential care placements for 60,000 children is £2.2 billion per year.

How well are we doing?

1.7 Over the last generation, children's lives have undergone profound change. Children have more opportunities than ever before, and benefit from rising prosperity, opportunities to study longer and better health. However, they also face more uncertainties and risks: children face earlier exposure to sexual activity, drugs and alcohol. Family patterns are changing. There are more lone parents, more divorces and more women in paid employment all of which has made family life more complex.

These changes have come at a time when we better understand the importance of early influences on the development of values and behaviour.

Figure 1

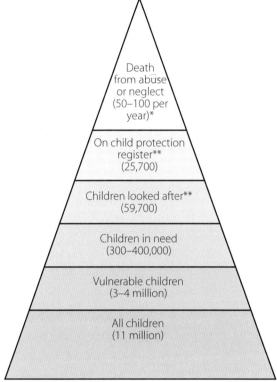

Death from abuse or neglect (50–100 per year)*

On child protection register** (25,700)

Children looked after** (59,700)

Children in need (300–400,000)

Vulnerable children (3–4 million)

All children (11 million)

* These children may not be on the child protection register, nor looked after, nor in need, nor vulnerable.
** These children are included in the children in need figure, and not all children on the child protection register are children looked after.

1.8 In recent years, there has been unprecedented investment and priority given to services for children to promote equal chances and to improve prevention and encourage early intervention. Key policy changes include:

● significant real terms rises in Child Benefit and more generous support through new tax credits. Child tax credits alone will provide £13 billion of support for families with children

● record investment in early years education for all children and childcare for children through Sure Start

● introduction of literacy and numeracy strategies in primary schools and extra support for schools in deprived areas through Excellence in Cities

● introduction of Quality Protects and the Children (Leaving Care) Act 2000

● the Children's Fund which supports local projects for 5 to 13 year olds and the Local Network Fund which invests in local community and voluntary groups working for and with children and young people aged 0-19

● the creation of Connexions to provide advice, guidance and personal development opportunities for young people aged 13-19

● the teenage pregnancy strategy and the wider Sexual Health and HIV Strategy

● the creation of Youth Offending Teams and the Youth Justice Board

● the updated Drugs Strategy published in December 2002, which will provide increased support for young people, especially those that are vulnerable

● an end to bed and breakfast accommodation for homeless families with children: new homelessness legislation treats 16 and 17 year olds not supported by social services as being vulnerable and in 'priority need' for accommodation.

Being healthy

Regular smoking by 11-15 year olds in England has decreased since 1996 from 13 to 10 percent. But levels of obesity are rising. Between 1996 and 2001 the proportion of obese children aged 6-15 years in England rose by 4 percent.

Teenage conception rates were 10 percent lower in 2001 than they were in 1998. But the UK still has the highest rate of teenage births within Western Europe.

In 2002 the World Health Organisation reported that the UK had the lowest rate of suicide amongst 26 countries. However, suicide still accounts for a fifth of deaths amongst our young people.

Staying safe

There were 59,700 children in care in England in March 2002, an increase of 22 percent since March 1994. However, numbers on child protection registers in England have been falling. At 31 March 2002 there were 25,700. Ten years previously, the number was 38,600.

Between 1981 and 2001 the proportion of juvenile males in England and Wales cautioned or convicted of an offence fell from 70 per 1,000 juvenile males in the population to 51 per 1,000. However, the equivalent rate for females rose from 13 to 14 per 1,000.

A study of offending and victimisation amongst 11 to 16 year olds in mainstream schools found that almost half (46 percent) reported being the victim of some kind of offence in the last 12 months.

Up to one in ten women experience domestic violence each year; in 90 percent of incidents, children are in the same or next room, and one in three child protection cases shows a history of domestic violence against the mother.

Enjoying and achieving

Since 1997 the proportion of 11 year olds achieving the expected level in English and maths for their age has increased by 12 percentage points, from 63 percent to 75 percent in English and from 61 percent to 73 percent in maths.

In 2002 over 51 percent of 15 year olds gained at least five GCSEs at grades A*-C, an increase of over 6 percentage points since 1997. But achievement is not consistent across different ethnic groups: students from Chinese and Indian backgrounds achieve significantly above average GCSE results; black pupils and those from Pakistani and Bangladeshi backgrounds achieve poorer GCSE results.

Unauthorised absence has remained constant since 1995/96 at 0.7 percent of half days missed.

One in eleven young people aged 16-18 years were not in education, employment or training at the end of 2001 and one in four young people spend some time outside education, training and work between 16 and 18.

Making a positive contribution

A recent study of secondary pupils aged 11 to 18 found that all but 14 percent had participated in some form of community activity in the past year – 50 percent had taken part in fundraising or collecting money for charity.

Estimates from the 2001 General Election suggest turnout was lowest among 18-24 year olds, with just two in five voting.

Economic well-being

Between 1992 and 1995 the proportion of children living in working age workless households was broadly constant at 19 percent. By 2003, the proportion had fallen to 15.2 percent in 2003.

The proportion of children living in households with relative low incomes fell between 1996-97 and 2001-02 from 34 percent to 30 percent after housing costs. The proportion of children living in households with absolute low incomes showed a large fall from 34 percent to 20 percent after housing costs.

1.9 There are strong signs that these policies are delivering progress. However, as the box above shows, while the vast majority of children thrive there is still a very wide range of experiences. The death of Victoria Climbié showed that children can still suffer the most appalling neglect and abuse, and that services can fail them, sometimes with tragic consequences.

What shapes outcomes?

1.10 We have a good idea what factors shape children's life chances. Research tells us that the risk of experiencing negative outcomes is concentrated in children with certain characteristics and experiences. Although research has not built up a detailed picture of the causal links, certain factors are associated with poor outcomes including:[ii]

- low income and parental unemployment
- homelessness
- poor parenting
- poor schooling
- post-natal depression among mothers
- low birth weight
- substance misuse
- individual characteristics such as intelligence
- community factors, such as living in a disadvantaged neighbourhood.

1.11 Outcomes also vary by race and gender. Underachievement and school exclusion are particularly concentrated in certain ethnic groups. Boys have higher rates of offending and exclusion, while self-harm and eating disorders are more prevalent among girls.

1.12 The more risk factors a child experiences, such as being excluded from school and family breakdown, the more likely it is that they will experience further negative outcomes.[iii] Research suggests that parenting appears to be the most important factor associated with educational attainment at age 10, which in turn is strongly associated with achievement later in life. Parental involvement in education seems to be a more important influence than poverty, school environment and the influence of peers.

1.13 A range of protective factors can help children overcome disadvantage including:[iv]

- strong relationships with parents, family members and other significant adults

- parental interest and involvement in education with clear and high expectations

- positive role models

- individual characteristics such as an outgoing nature, self-motivation, intelligence

- active involvement in family, school and community life

- recognition, praise and feeling valued.

1.14 Children are particularly affected by their experience during the early years before they reach school age. As Figure 2 below shows, even at 22 months, there is a big gap between the development of children from different socio-economic groups. Other research shows that the academic results of boys are particularly

Figure 2: The socio-economic position of parents affects children from a very early age

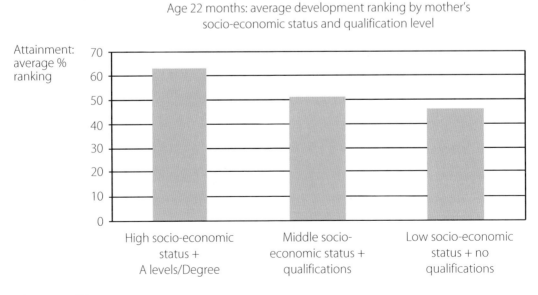

Age 22 months: average development ranking by mother's socio-economic status and qualification level

Source: Feinstein, 1999.[vi]

Figure 3

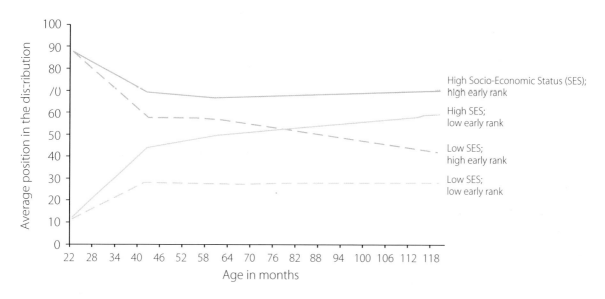

Source: Feinstein, Economica (2003)

affected if their mother has suffered from post-natal depression. Teenagers who were severely underweight at birth achieve lower GCSE grades than their peers.[v]

1.15 When children enter primary school, children from poorer backgrounds start to fall behind children from higher income families. As Figure 3 shows, children from a poor background with a high developmental score at 22 months have fallen behind by the age of 10, compared to children from higher socio-economic groups but with a low developmental score at 22 months.

Figure 4: Continuity of anti-social behaviour from age 5 to 17

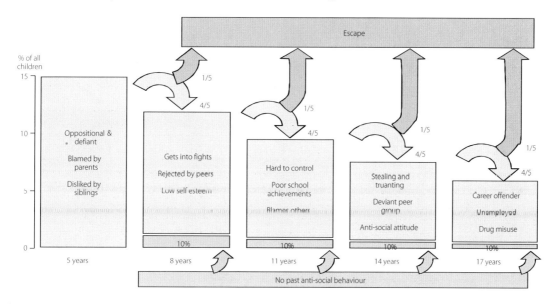

Source: Scott 2002

Research conducted by Stephen Scott for Home Office, 2002 (unpublished).

Figure 5: The transition from primary to secondary school

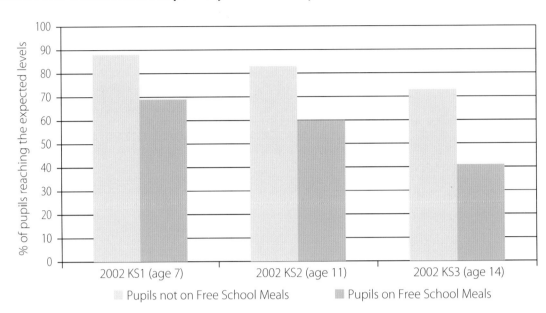

Notes: The expected level is the average of reading, writing and maths at KS1 and English, maths and science at KS2 and KS3

Source: 2002 Provisonal results from the National Pupil Database

1.16 Although experience during the early years is important, life chances continue to be forged throughout children's lives. Problems can build up cumulatively over time reinforcing disadvantage, as Figure 4 shows.

1.17 A critical transition is from primary to secondary school and the onset of puberty. As Figure 5 shows, the gap in educational achievement between higher and lower socio-economic groups opens up starkly in the first years of secondary school from 11 to 14.

Policy challenges

1.18 The implications of this analysis are that there needs to be:

- **better prevention.** We need to tackle the key drivers of poor outcomes, including poverty, poor childcare and early years education, poor schooling and

lack of access to health services. By mainstreaming preventative approaches, such as those developed through Sure Start, we ought to reduce the numbers of children requiring more intensive support. Support need to be provided throughout the lifecycle, with increasing attention focused on two critical periods: the early years, and the beginning of secondary school as children experience puberty. Services need to focus particularly on addressing inequalities across gender and ethnicity

- **a stronger focus on parenting and families.** We need to pay more attention to the critical relationships between children and their families and provide them with better support. We should recognise the vital role played by fathers as well as mothers. When children cannot remain with their birth parents, we need to ensure they can develop stable, loving relationships with carers

● **earlier intervention.** We need a greater focus on ensuring children at risk are identified earlier. We need to be able to share information to identify children who require additional support, and provide a tailored service that safeguards them from abuse and neglect, and enables them to fulfil their potential.

1.19 To deliver these reforms, we need to address two underlying challenges, highlighted by the Victoria Climbié Inquiry Report, and other studies:

● **weak accountability and poor integration.** Our existing system for supporting children and young people who are beginning to experience difficulties is often poorly co-ordinated and accountability is unclear. This means that information is not shared between agencies so that warning signs are not recognised and acted upon. Some children are assessed many times by different agencies and despite this may get no services. Children may experience a range of professionals involved in their lives but little continuity and consistency of support. Organisations may disagree over who should pay for meeting a

Figure 6: Targeted services within a universal context

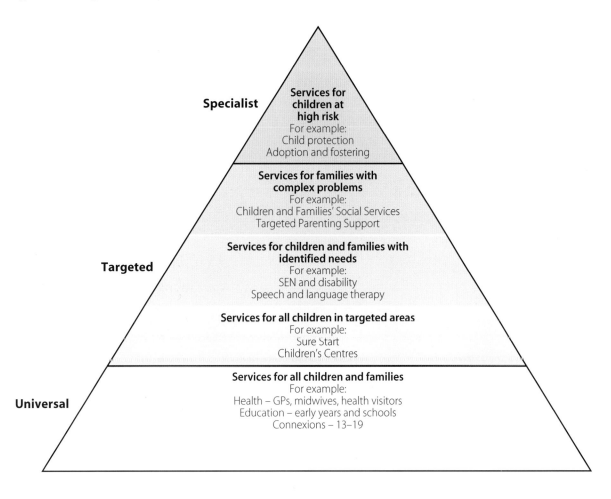

Specialist

Services for children at high risk
For example:
Child protection
Adoption and fostering

Services for families with complex problems
For example:
Children and Families' Social Services
Targeted Parenting Support

Targeted

Services for children and families with identified needs
For example:
SEN and disability
Speech and language therapy

Services for all children in targeted areas
For example:
Sure Start
Children's Centres

Universal

Services for all children and families
For example:
Health – GPs, midwives, health visitors
Education – early years and schools
Connexions – 13–19

child's needs because their problems cut across organisational boundaries. Fragmentation locally is often driven by conflicting messages and competing priorities from central Government.

● **workforce reform.** We need to do more to ensure working with children is seen as an attractive career, and improve skills and inter-professional relationships. Many of those who work with children and young people in vital frontline roles feel undervalued, and in some cases under siege. Problems are most acute in social work, where there is an 11 percent vacancy rate nationally (as high as 40–50 percent in some London boroughs). Some professionals working with children have no routine training in child development, child protection or domestic violence issues and frontline staff often lack awareness of specialist issues like mental health, special educational needs and substance misuse.

1.20 The following Chapters examine in more detail how the five challenges set out above will be addressed.

i   Scott, Stephen et al *Financial costs of social exclusion: follow up study of antisocial children into adulthood*, British Medical Journal, July 2001; 323:191.

ii Department for Education and Skills, *Participation in education, training and employment by 16-18 year olds in England 2000 and 2001* Statistical First Release 16/2002.

iii Bynner, J *Childhood Risks and Protective Factors in Social Exclusion*, Children and Society, 2001, vol.15, pp.285-301.

iv Joseph Rowntree Foundation, *A National Survey of Problem Behaviour and Associated Risk and Protective Factors Among Young People* (April 2002).

v   Feinstein, Birth Cohort Study (1999).

vi Feinstein, Birth Cohort Study (1999).

Strong Foundations

Over the last six years, the Government has put in place strong foundations to improve services for children and young people. This Chapter sets out our commitment to build on these achievements to meet the needs of all children and young people through:

- **tackling child poverty**

- **ensuring children have a Sure Start**

- **raising primary and secondary school standards and participation in post 16 learning**

- **increasing access to primary health care and specialist health services**

- **reducing offending and anti-social behaviour**

- **building strong and vibrant communities**

- **ensuring children are safe.**

Child poverty

2.1 The Government is committed to halving child poverty by 2010, and eradicating it by 2020. The best way to tackle child poverty is to widen opportunities for parents to work, and raise the incomes of working families. To achieve this, the Government is:

- helping parents enter work through the New Deal

- removing the barriers to work through widening access to childcare

- ensuring work pays through the national minimum wage and the introduction of tax credits for working families.

2.2 In addition, the Government has increased financial support for all families with children in recognition of the costs and responsibilities that come with parenthood.

2.3 Those who need greatest support receive the most help, including families on lower incomes, those with children under one, and parents of disabled children. The new Child Tax Credit plays a key part in the Government's strategy to tackle child poverty, providing a single system of income-related support for families with children.

2

Ensuring children have a Sure Start

2.4 The period from conception through to the start of school is critical to later life chances. The Government aims to extend the principles developed in Sure Start local programmes across other services. These principles focus on: working with parents and children; starting very early and being flexible at the point of delivery; providing services for everyone and ensuring services are community driven, professionally co-ordinated across agencies and outcome focused. The Government is building on the introduction of Sure Start and the National Childcare Strategy through further investment over the next three years.

Improved access to ante and post-natal care

2.5 The most vulnerable women are more likely to delay seeking care when pregnant and to fail to attend clinics regularly. Through the Government's National Service Framework for Children[i] and other policies, the Government is:

- creating more accessible primary care, for instance, through walk-in centres and the expansion of Sure Start

- looking at standards for improving access to maternity services and improving the identification of and services for post-natal depression

- exploring how health visitor services can be more closely integrated with other community services for families and provide support to families in greatest need

- piloting routine ante-natal questioning for domestic violence.

Sure Start Children's Centres, early years and childcare

2.6 The Government is establishing a network of Sure Start Children's Centres in disadvantaged areas, offering integrated early education and full day care, health services, and family and parenting support. These will reach pre-school children in the 20 percent poorest wards by March 2006. Children's Centres will play a key role in supporting groups who are at risk as well as delivering mainstream childcare and education services.

2.7 Children's Centres will signpost families to other services and facilities, for example local play spaces, childcare for older children and children's information services. Children's Centres will play a key role in communities alongside schools and general practitioners as a focus for parents and children to access services.

2.8 The Government is also increasing the amount of childcare and out of school care in all areas, including at least 1,150,000 new childcare places by 2006, start up support for childcare providers, and funding for sustaining childcare provision in disadvantaged areas. In addition to this, we will be shortly extending free part time education, currently available for all four year olds, to all three year olds.

Better early years support for disabled children

2.9 Early identification of learning difficulties or disabilities can be vital to a child's learning and life chances. In some areas, major breakthroughs have recently been made. In particular, the screening of newborn babies means that deafness and hearing problems can now be diagnosed months or years earlier than in the past.

2.10 The Government has been working with the voluntary sector, the National Health Service, local authorities and others to set in place an Early Support Pilot Programme to support families of very young disabled children. We are evaluating lessons from this programme with a view to extending aspects of the Early Support Pilot Programme across the country.[ii]

Raising primary and secondary school standards and participation in post 16 learning

2.11 Excellent education is vital to the lives of vulnerable children. The Government has recently set out plans for the reform of the primary and secondary education system to ensure high standards for all pupils[iii]. This section looks at measures to improve school attendance and behaviour, improve outcomes for children with special educational needs, ensure more children stay on in education or training after 16, and integrate services through extended schools and clusters of schools.

Improving school attendance and behaviour

2.12 Through the national behaviour and attendance strategy, the Government is implementing a number of measures:

- providing key workers for every child at risk through projects in schools in 61 authorities

- creating multi-agency Behaviour and Education Support Teams working with a cluster of schools to help those pupils with the most serious problems

- from September 2003, providing training and support to all secondary schools in England in behaviour and attendance as part of the Key Stage 3 Strategy, and piloting similar work in primary schools in 25 local education authorities (LEAs)

- providing intensive support to 56 LEAs with high levels of truancy

- increasing the numbers of learning mentors and learning support units

- ensuring nationally co-ordinated truancy sweeps take place regularly

- implementing the Fast Track to Prosecution initiative

- through the Anti-Social Behaviour Bill, providing all local education authorities and schools with additional tools, such as penalty notices and parenting contracts, with which to tackle truancy.

2.13 For children who are permanently excluded from schools, the Government will maintain the full time provision that is now in place for all excluded pupils. We must ensure that alternative provision is effective, appropriate and of good quality. We will also ensure that by 2005 there are systems in place in every local authority to identify and maintain contact with children who might miss education; and that by 2006, all children identified as missing education or at risk of doing so receive a full time education appropriate to their needs.

Raising the attainment of minority ethnic pupils

2.14 There is evidence to show that the performance of pupils from certain minority ethnic backgrounds lags considerably behind that of their peers. Through a national strategy for raising the attainment of minority ethnic pupils, the Government will:

- develop the leadership capacity in schools to deliver a whole school approach to raising achievement

- provide teachers with knowledge and skills and support them to close achievement gaps

- develop strategies for supporting bilingual learners

- develop strategies for addressing the low achievement levels of African-Caribbean pupils and reducing levels of exclusion

- use resources more effectively to support the achievement of minority ethnic pupils.

Special educational needs

2.15 The Government has made improvements to the law to give young people with special educational needs (SEN) and disabilities a stronger right to a place in mainstream school and to extend the protection of the Disability Discrimination Act to education.

2.16 Our focus now is on improving educational outcomes for all children. While the statutory framework provides important assurances, the processes involved can be time-consuming, bureaucratic and frustrating for parents and children alike, and there remain wide variations in levels of service provision across the country.

2.17 We are tackling these problems through the development of an SEN Action Programme. The Action Programme will focus on practical measures to promote early identification and intervention for children with SEN, raise expectations and achievement and build the capacity of schools and early years settings, working with health and social care, to provide good teaching and support for all children. Our aim is to ensure that parents have the confidence that their children's needs will be met quickly and effectively throughout their education without feeling that the only way to achieve this is through a statement.

Education and training in the teenage years

2.18 The Government is committed to ensuring more young people stay on in education and training until they are 19 and make a successful transition to adulthood. To achieve this we are:

- creating a more flexible curriculum from 14-19 to respond to individual needs and aspirations, with improved vocational options and better individual planning from the end of Key Stage 3

- developing the Connexions service, which provides information and support for 13-19 year olds. It helps young people stay engaged in education, training and employment. For those who need it, it provides intensive support from a personal adviser. With the young person, that adviser can develop an individual package of learning and remove barriers to achievement, addressing such issues as housing needs and financial support

- implementing nationally the Education Maintenance Allowance to provide all 16-19 year olds from low income backgrounds in full time education with up to £30 a week

- ensuring that every child will be granted a Child Trust Fund with an initial endowment at birth of £250, rising to £500 for children in the poorest third of families

- reviewing financial support for 16-19 year olds to examine the incentives for young people to stay in education and training financial support for young people and their carers, including those living independently and those in very low-paid employment; and how the system of financial support might be rationalised.

2.19 For young people leaving care, we have made a significant start through the Children (Leaving Care) Act 2000. This puts stronger duties on local authorities to support care leavers until they are 21. The trend for young people to leave care at 16 has been reversed. For disabled young people, and those with learning difficulties, we will take steps to improve the transition to adulthood through the National Service Framework for Children, the SEN Action Programme, and the work of Connexions.

Integrating services through extended schools and clusters of schools

2.20 The Government wants to integrate education, health and social care services around the needs of children. To achieve this, we want all schools to become extended schools – acting as the hub for services for children, families and other members of the community. Extended schools offer the community and their pupils a range of services (such as childcare, adult learning, health and community facilities) that go beyond their core educational function.

2.21 The Government is also creating a network of full service extended schools, with at least one in every LEA in England by 2006. Each full service school will offer a core of childcare, study support, family and lifelong learning, health and social care, parenting support, sports and arts facilities, and access to Information Technology. By 2006, all LEAs will also be funded to employ school based managers or LEA co-ordinators to develop more services for children and to be provided in school buildings.

Increasing access to primary health care and specialist health services

2.22 The new national standards developed through the National Service Framework for Children (NSF) will help to ensure better access and smoother progression in the provision of services for children, from initial contact with the NHS, via a GP surgery or NHS hospital, through to social services support.

2.23 Over the past year, expert working groups have been set up to focus on: the health of all children; maternity services; child and adolescent mental health services; disabled children; children in special circumstances; hospital and acute services; and medicines. These themes will be taken forward as the NSF is finalised, along with the development of a range of toolkits to support implementation.

Primary health care

2.24 GPs and the primary health care team are the cornerstone of family health care for the vast majority of children. There are over 10,000 surgeries, many within 'pram-pushing distance' of deprived communities. The Government has a range of policies to improve access to primary care, to increase the range of services available outside hospital settings and to reduce health inequalities. Key developments include:

- the new General Medical Services contract will improve the quality of services for children. We want to ensure that clinicians in primary care have extra training to develop their expertise to

deliver more specialised care with children without requiring a hospital visit. Most of those receiving extra training are currently GPs, but many nurses and others will also develop special skills

- the links between primary care services and their local communities will need to be preserved and enhanced in future years. The development of connections between Children's Centres, Children's Trusts (see Chapter Five) and General Practice will be critical to ensuring continuity of care, information sharing and effective support for children at risk.

Specialist health services

2.25 There are a range of specialist health services that are critical to supporting children, particularly those with acute needs, or who require therapeutic services.

Speech and Language Therapy

2.26 Action has been taken to increase the number of speech and language training places by 31 percent between 1998/9 and 2002/3.

2.27 However, there are still capacity constraints leading to long waits for some young children to access services. Work on the forthcoming NSF is looking at how to tackle this, including through support from specialist services and training para-professionals and assistants. In addition, local commissioners of services need to use the increased investment in services for children to develop effective ways of building capacity in specialist interventions.

Mental health services

2.28 Over the next three years the NHS and social care will work together to increase capacity by ten percent each year for the next three years and to broaden their services, so that all areas are delivering a comprehensive Child and Adolescent Mental Health Service (CAMHS) by 2006.

2.29 A comprehensive service should cover a diverse range of services appropriate to the age and circumstances of children and young people, and to their different levels of need. For example:

● people working in universal services should be able to identify children who may need help, and offer advice and support to those with mild problems

● trained mental health workers need to be able to support workers in other agencies. Specialist multi-disciplinary teams should be able to provide assessment and treatment, and short and long term interventions and care

● services may need to be located in a range of settings, as near as possible to home in environments which are perceived as less stigmatising than traditional clinic settings, such as schools, homes and family centres.

2.30 To achieve this, it will be essential to develop high quality commissioning of mental health services that takes into account the needs of groups for whom there is currently poor or no provision, including children with learning disabilities, autistic spectrum disorders, minority ethnic groups,

children and young people who need in-patient care, children with behavioural problems, and those in the criminal justice system. To develop better knowledge of users' needs, it will be important to use creative approaches to consult users of CAMHS about their views.

2.31 The full NSF, published next year, will build on the NSF emerging findings to set national standards for the delivery of services to meet the needs of children and young people with mental health problems.

Sexual health

2.32 The Government's National Strategy for Sexual Health and HIV published in 2001 set out a ten year programme of investment and reform to modernise sexual health services and reduce unintended pregnancy rates and sexually transmitted infections (STIs), and to improve services for people with HIV.[iv]

2.33 Our new mass media safer sex campaign should improve awareness of STIs and how to avoid them. We have also started rolling out the chlamydia screening programme. We are investing £10 million in genito-urinary medicine services this year, which will deliver shorter waiting times for urgent appointments and improved access to services.

Substance misuse

2.34 The Government's objective is to reduce the use of Class A drugs and the frequent use of any illicit drug amongst all young people under the age of 25 and especially by the most vulnerable young people.[v]

2.35 Education has an important role to play in delivering this target. We are providing funding to local education authorities to expand and improve the quality of drugs education in schools and we have launched a major awareness raising campaign – FRANK – to increase young people's understanding of the risks and dangers associated with Class A drugs.

2.36 We know that some children are more at risk of substance misuse than others, including those that are looked after, homeless, truants and young offenders. We are therefore providing funding to Primary Care Trusts, local authorities, Connexions Partnerships and Youth Offending Teams to target these vulnerable groups.

2.37 However, we recognise that there is still more work to be done. We are keen to improve services in two particular areas:

- children's services commissioners should ensure that the full range of substance misuse work from education through to prevention and treatment is embedded in mainstream services

- all professionals working with children and young people should be able to identify, assess and undertake appropriate action for addressing substance misuse issues. In order to enable them to do this effectively, training on substance misuse should form part of initial and ongoing professional development.

Building strong and vibrant communities

2.38 The communities in which children and their families live have a fundamental impact on their lives. Children who grow up in communities scarred by crime and violence, and lacking safe activities, are severely disadvantaged.

2.39 A consistent theme of consultations with children and young people is the importance of having communities where there is 'somewhere safe to go and something to do'. This not only provides recreational activity for children and young people, but helps build the fabric of communities and increases young people's skills, confidence and self-esteem.

2.40 The Government intends to widen access to a range of structured and unstructured, supervised and unsupervised, activities. We are supporting this goal through:

- **investment in youth services.** The Government has made £513 million available this year to local authority youth services – an average increase of 5.9 percent. In return for this, local authorities are expected to meet the national standards for youth work and provide a pledge to young people about the services that can expect in their area.[vi]

- **Positive Activities for Young People (PAYP) programme.** This new programme is aimed at those young people most at risk of anti-social behaviour, offending or truanting. The new national programme covers all school holiday periods. £25 million is being provided for the first year with a view to extending the programme for a further two years

- **Young People's Fund.** An initial budget of £200 million has been allocated to the Fund from the Lottery with the view to establishing it as an ongoing source of funding. The views of local young people will be sought when deciding what money should be used for in their area

- **PE and school sport.** The national strategy for PE, school sport and club links is aimed at enhancing the take-up of sporting opportunities by 5-16 year olds. The Government has a commitment to increase the percentage of school children who spend a minimum of two hours each week on high quality PE and school sport within and beyond the curriculum to 75 percent by 2006.[vii] Between 2003 and 2006, the Government is investing £459 million to transform PE and school sport, on top of £686 million to improve school sport facilities across England.

2.41 In order to maximise the effectiveness of these resources, Government will look to local authorities to ensure there is an effective system for identifying and prioritising needs more effectively and signposting opportunities to children, young people and families.

Anti-social and offending behaviour

2.42 When children and young people engage in anti-social behaviour or commit offences, we need to ensure that they to face up to their actions and redress the harm they have caused. We also need to ensure that the system tackles the underlying causes of such behaviour.

2.43 The Government would like to build on the success of recent youth justice reforms by making the system clearer and simpler, and making more use of effective interventions known to work. Details of the youth justice proposals are published alongside this Green Paper. Key measures include:

- ensuring that there are more effective powers to intervene positively to address the behaviour of children under 10 who commit what would be offences if they were over the age of criminal responsibility. This includes revising the Child Safety Order, and revising the breach provisions so that proceedings for a Care Order would no longer be available as a breach penalty

- making the Intensive Supervision and Surveillance Programme the main intervention for those who would otherwise have to go into custody

- rationalising the number of community sentences to create a new simplified 'menu' community sentence. Simplification would make the youth justice process easier to understand for those sentencing, for lawyers and for defendants. It would allow magistrates the flexibility to select a package of interventions individually tailored to the needs of each young person. The menu will include provision for drugs treatment, anger management, parenting programmes and restorative justice

- building on policy set out in the recent Home Office White Paper *Respect and Responsibility: taking a stand against anti-social behaviour*, we propose making greater use of a wider range of imaginative residential placements for young offenders, such as intensive fostering, including for 10 and 11 year old persistent offenders

- we also plan to make use of junior attendance centres by developing them into broader junior activity centres. This will give magistrates a flexible facility to support community sentences, particularly at weekends.

Ensuring children are safe

Tackling bullying

2.44 The Government is developing a range of services to tackle bullying in school through:

- ensuring every school has an anti-bullying policy that has involved children in its development and implementation[viii]

- continuing work on Safer Schools Partnerships which place police in schools, who work with children and young people at risk of becoming victims and offenders and support school staff in dealing with incidents of crime and anti-social behaviour

- ensuring that personal, health and social education (PHSE), citizenship education and the National Healthy Schools Standard help children develop good relationships, learn about conflict resolution and encourage them to take responsibility for their own actions and to support their fellow pupils.

Supporting victims

2.45 In addition, the Government is taking a range of measures to protect children and young people who suffer as victims:

- support for young victims and witnesses going through the criminal justice system, including the early assessment of their needs and the provision of support and information, as well as improvements in the provision of special measures, such as separate entrances to court buildings and facilities for providing evidence via video link

- building on existing models of best practice when dealing with children who become involved in prostitution, encouraging inter-agency working. This will involve a focus on treating these young people as victims, rather than offenders

- making it easier to bring those who exploit them to justice by creating a new offence of commercial sexual exploitation of a child. This will protect children up to the age of 18 and will cover buying the sexual services of a child, coercing a child into sexual exploitation, facilitating the commercial sexual exploitation of a child and controlling the activities of a child involved in prostitution or pornography.

Children and young people suffering from homelessness

2.46 Meeting the support needs of homeless families with children presents particular challenges since such families can rapidly become disconnected from services.

2.47 The Homelessness Act 2002 requires local authorities to conduct a review of homelessness in their area and put in place a strategy by July 2003 to tackle and prevent homelessness. In addition the Homelessness (Priority Need) Order extended the groups for which local authorities must give priority need for accommodation to include young people leaving care, 16 and 17 year olds not supported by social services, and other vulnerable people.

2.48 To build on this, the Government has set a target that by March 2004 no homeless family with children should be placed in bed and breakfast accommodation, unless in a short term emergency and is consulting on eliminating the use of bed and breakfast accommodation for families with children from April 2004.

2.49 The Government is currently consulting on standards for temporary accommodation and proposals to produce clear guidance on the arrangements that should be put in place to ensure that all households, including families with children, placed in temporary accommodation by housing authorities under the legislation

receive support to ensure that their health, education and social services needs are met.

Supporting children entering the country

2.50 Some of the children in greatest need are unaccompanied asylum seekers. They may have left their homes and communities in violent and traumatic circumstances and be in poor health. Unaccompanied asylum-seeking children now represent approximately 6 percent of all children in care, mainly concentrated in London and the South East.

2.51 The Government will seek to invest more in training for immigration officers to improve their identification of children at risk and help them respond appropriately. We will also build on existing initiatives which enable greater joint working between the Immigration Service, social services and the police, such as co-locating child protection police officers at ports.

2.52 Children would often benefit from well managed care in a part of the country better able to support them. A pilot safe case transfer scheme is underway, which ensures that unaccompanied asylum-seeking children reach partner local authorities outside the South East with a package of support and reception prepared for them.

2.53 The resources provided for the support of unaccompanied children have increased over the last few years. In particular, the Refugee Council's Children's Panel plays an important role in helping children through the asylum determination process and in accessing the services that they need for inclusion. However, they are only able to provide support to a minority of children. We would welcome views on how to provide more comprehensive and consistent support for unaccompanied asylum-seeking children, building on the work of the Children's Panel.

2.54 The Government recognises that we need to increase our capacity to support children who have been trafficked to the UK against their will. There is a need for close co-operation between all the key agencies, in particular police, immigration and social services, in order to protect children from their traffickers and develop intelligence to disrupt the trafficking networks. Joint working protocols have been developed at certain key entry points, and it is important that work of this kind is further extended. The publication of a trafficking toolkit, a best practice guide, has helped to raise awareness of these issues and provide practical support for agencies that may come into contact with potential victims.[ix] The new offences in the Sex Offences Bill will provide for tough 14 year prison terms for child trafficking and sexual exploitation.

---

i   The Government is developing a National Service Framework for children's health and social services. The NSF is a ten-year programme intended to stimulate long-term and sustained improvement in care.

ii   More details on the early support pilots can be found at (www.esp.org.uk). The Government has published guidance relating to this, 'Together From the Start' (www.doh.gov.uk/nsf/children/togetherindex.htm).

iii More details on primary and secondary education reforms are set out in *Excellence and Enjoyment and A New Specialist System: Transforming Secondary Education.*

iv   For more details on how the Government is building on this, please see the National Service Framework for Children and the Government's recent document Tackling Health Inequalities.

v   For more details, see the updated *Drugs Strategy 2002.*

vi   For more details, see *Transforming Youth Work: Resourcing Excellent Youth Services*, Department for Education and Skills, 2002

vii Eight underpinning programmes will achieve this by establishing a national infrastructure for PE and school sport, raising the aspirations and performance of those with talent, improving the quality of teaching and learning, encouraging involvement in sports leadership and volunteering, enhancing links between schools and sports clubs and ensuring that more primary-age children can swim.

viii To help schools create policies that work the Government has produced guidance, a video and online support (www.dfes.gov.uk/bullying/).

ix   The toolkit is available online at www.crimereduction.gov.uk/toolkits

Consultation Questions

Views are invited on the proposals set out in this Chapter. In particular:

- How can we improve support for unaccompanied asylum-seeking children, building on the work of the Children's Panel?

- How can we ensure that serious welfare concerns are appropriately dealt with alongside criminal proceedings?

- How can we encourage clusters of schools to work together around extended schools?

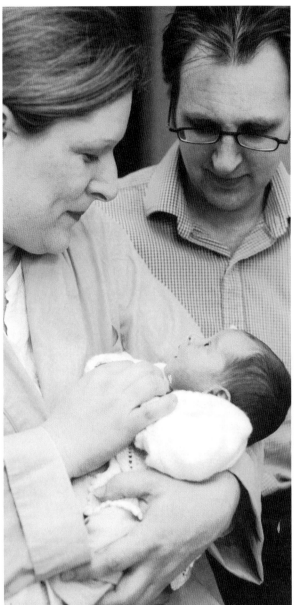

Supporting Parents and Carers

The Government intends to put supporting parents and carers at the heart of its approach to improving children's lives. The Green Paper consults on a long term vision to improve parenting and family support through:

- **universal services** such as schools, health services and childcare providing information and advice and engaging parents in supporting their child's development, where such support is needed or wanted

- **targeted and specialist** support to parents of children requiring additional support

- **compulsory action** through Parenting Orders as a last resort where parents are condoning a child's anti-social behaviour such as truancy or offending.

All children deserve the chance to grow up in a loving secure family. Through the adoption modernisation programme,

local authorities are already delivering significant increases in adoption of looked after children. The Adoption and Children Act 2002 will further strengthen this programme of reform. The Green Paper consults on measures to tackle the recruitment and retention challenges in **foster care**, and to ensure that foster carers have the skills and support they need to care for vulnerable children.

Why parenting matters

3.1 The bond between the child and their parents is the most critical influence on a child's life. Parenting has a strong impact on a child's educational development, behaviour, and mental health.

3.2 In the past, public policy has paid insufficient attention to supporting parents and helping families find solutions for themselves. By bringing policy on parenting and family support into the Department for Education and Skills, alongside policy on children, the Government has put it at the heart of children's services.

Universal parenting services

3.3 Based on existing practice, the Government would like to develop more and better universal services, open to all families as and when they need them. This could include:

- a **national helpline** or 'virtual advice bureau for parents' which would offer immediate advice and help and would signpost parents towards local help and support. This could build on the experience of the voluntary and community organisations in delivering such services

INSPIRE is a Birmingham LEA initiative which involves parents in schools and in children's learning in order to: build the confidence of parents and schools to work more effectively together; increase parental involvement in literacy and numeracy at home; and raise the literacy and numeracy standards achieved by children. Parents, extended family members or even neighbours are invited by the child to sit side by side with them and the teacher for practical activities such as producing a game, song, stories, puppets or books.

More than 300 primary schools in Birmingham are involved and evidence shows over 40,000 parents involved each year, including some groups who have been hard to engage, such as men and some minority ethnic families.

After the first year, 73 percent of schools reported increased educational activity in the home, and 88 percent reported increased parental understanding of the child's learning in the classroom.

School-Home Support is a voluntary organisation working in over 100 schools providing school based, school-home support workers to help parents support their children in education. In one project, two workers are employed to support in particular Turkish and Kurdish parents across two primary schools on the border of Islington and Hackney. They encourage parents to participate in English as a Second Language (ESOL) classes and to take on voluntary roles within the community.

The Spokes Project is an intensive course in primary schools aimed at reducing anti-social behaviour and improving reading skills. The first term addresses the parent-child relationship and how to handle difficult behaviour. The second term comprises a ten week reading programme, and the two elements are then combined in a six week course in the third term. Children's social behaviour is shown to have improved as a result and their reading level increased by seven months.

- **parents' information meetings** at **key transition points** in their children's lives (such as the move from primary to secondary school). Led by trained peers or professionals these would provide information about child development, learning and behaviour as well as direct parents towards specific help

- **family learning programmes** bringing family members together to work and learn on a planned activity. These programmes focus on engaging parents in their children's development and offer opportunities to increase involvement in learning, to break down barriers between school and parents, and act as a link to targeted help and support

- **support programmes for fathers as well as mothers** so that all children, but especially those who are living apart from their fathers, develop positive relationships with both parents

- ensuring **better communication between parents and schools** to help support children to learn. We need to look at opportunities for families, and especially fathers, to become more closely involved in school life through parents' associations, as school governors, and as a result of home-school contracts

- **childcare, early years education, social care and schools** working more closely with parents to strengthen their understanding of how to help their child's development

- **joint training on development and behaviour issues** for children's professionals so they can provide initial support for parents and signpost those with particular needs to targeted services

Specialist parenting support

3.4 In addition to services open to all parents, there needs to be a range of tailored help and support available for specific groups. The Government would welcome views on how local authorities working closely with the voluntary, community and private sectors can develop a menu of such services including:

- **home visiting programmes** consisting of frequent visits to parents in the pre- and post-natal period, supporting breastfeeding and the detection and management of post-natal depression, which have shown significant long term effects on child abuse and neglect, and on injury prevention

- **parent education programmes,** targeted particularly at the parents of 5-8 year olds, where existing programmes have been shown to have the largest impact on children's behaviour. These can involve at least six weekly sessions, where parents are trained in behavioural techniques

- **family group conferencing** to support families to get together and develop a plan with an independent facilitator, which may be triggered by child protection or youth offending concerns

> **Home Start is a home visiting programme in which trained parent volunteers, supported by paid staff, work with parents who have at least one child under five. Volunteers offer friendship, support and practical help to families in their own home, with a range of supporting activities including group work, outings, social events and toy libraries.**
>
> **Research into Home Start and other home visiting schemes confirms that they produce benefits for parents and children. Home Start raises self-confidence, improves social networks, reduces difficult behaviour on the part of the child, and improves physical and mental health.**

- **family mediation services**

- **stress and relationship counselling.**

3.5 Home Start currently operates 235 schemes, providing home visiting services to one in fifty families in each area. The Government intends to bring forward proposals to roll out nationally this level of targeted home visiting support provided through Home Start. We will work with local authorities and existing providers to identify and overcome obstacles to making home visiting services available more widely. In the longer term we will consider the balance between Home Start and the home visiting support provided through Sure Start local programmes and by organisations such as Community Mothers.

3.6 In addition, it is important to provide support to parents or carers who are facing particular difficulties because of their, or their children's, circumstances and experiences.

Parent and carers of disabled children

3.7 As part of the National Service Framework for Children (NSF), the Government is considering how best to support the particular needs of families with disabled children, who require flexible services responsive to their particular circumstances and needs. Through the introduction of direct payments, which enable local authorities to give families the funds to buy the help they need, the Government is giving parents more choice over how they receive services.

3.8 Parents of disabled children have not made wide use of direct payments up to now. Some parents have said that they do not feel confident taking the responsibility of using direct payments to employ staff. Some local authorities are still reluctant to offer direct payments. The Government wants to see greater use of direct payments and would welcome views on what further action could be taken to extend the use of direct payments by families with disabled children.

Young carers

3.9 Another group of families who would benefit from targeted, sensitive help are those of young carers. There are around 150,000 young carers, a significant number of whom provide many hours of care every week. They may be obliged to take on quite inappropriate levels of responsibility at the expense of their childhood and their education. Often the young carers will be helped most effectively by support to their parents, to enable them to fulfil their own parenting role. The NSF will look at the needs of children in special circumstances, including young carers. As part of its teenage pregnancy strategy, the Government is also particularly keen to support teenage parents back into full time education, training and work, through providing free childcare.

Children with parents in prison

3.10 Seven percent of children during their time at school experience the imprisonment of a father, while every year, approximately 150,000 children have a parent who enters custody. Prisoners' families, including their children, often experience increased financial, emotional and health problems during a sentence. 30 percent of prisoners' children suffer significant mental health problems, compared with 10 percent of the general child population. During their sentence, 45 percent of offenders lose contact with their families, and many separate from their partners. In the longer term, there is a proven pattern of increased inter-generational offending associated with parental convictions.

3.11 There is nobody currently within prisons or among community services with responsibility for supporting families in maintaining links and overcoming their problems. Research with children has shown that they usually want to maintain links with their imprisoned parents, but they lack help and encounter many obstacles, especially in visiting prisons. A renewed focus has led to some improvements in recent years, and a number of schemes, mainly run by the voluntary sector, have emerged. However, support for the children and families of offenders still depends largely on local will and initiative. The Government would welcome views on what more could be done to improve services for this group.

Compulsory action with parents and families

3.12 Some parents will be harder to engage and their problems may be more entrenched. When persistent truanting or anti-social behaviour is condoned by parents, compulsory action may be needed to ensure parents meet their responsibilities. Recent research shows that parenting programmes can reduce reconviction rates among young offenders by 50 percent, and that nine out of ten parents would subsequently recommend the programme to other parents. The Anti-Social Behaviour White Paper sets out a series of measures aimed at supporting parents, building on the success of Parenting Orders.

The **Webster-Stratton parent training programme** is a 13 to 16 week course targeted at children with conduct behaviour disorders. The costs per hour of contact with family are half those of the costs of standard clinical treatment. The programme has resulted in a large reduction in children's anti-social behaviour including hitting, running away, and fighting with siblings and has significantly reduced hyperactivity. 51 out of 67 Child and Adolescent Mental Health Services now offer parent training programmes.

The **Marlborough Family Service Education Unit** runs a programme to tackle barriers to learning by focusing on repeating cycles of disruptive behaviour. Each child has measurable behavioural targets on areas such as anger and stress management, which are rated every day by parents, class teachers and pupils themselves.

3.13 The Government recognises that there are significant constraints to increasing family support. Over time it will be important to ensure the increases in mainstream spending through social services, primary care, youth justice and education are harnessed to improve support for parents. In addition, the Government has introduced a £25 million Parenting Fund to build better support for parents and families through the voluntary and community sector. To reinforce this, as part of the next Spending Review, we shall encourage local and national funding bodies to offer longer term funding, simplify applications processes and streamline administrative burdens.

Improving Fostering and Adoption services

3.14 The vast majority of children will receive safe and effective care from their parents. Other children are less fortunate and the state may need to intervene in family life. The Government's first objective for children's social services is to ensure that all children are securely attached to carers capable of providing safe and effective care for the duration of their childhood.[ii]

3.15 Every child needs to feel secure within a loving family. In practice this means strong attachments to adults who are committed to them long term, who support their development and who guide their transition through childhood to adulthood.

3.16 Most children who are looked after eventually return home, and almost one in three return home within eight weeks. For children who are unable to return home quickly, timely and purposeful decisions must be made about where they will live in the future. We call this planning for permanence.

Care Planning and Reviews

An effective care plan will include a plan for permanence for the child, while setting objectives for work with the child, birth family and carers in relation to the child's developmental needs. Care planning and reviewing is not static but rather a process of continuous monitoring and reassessment. Review meetings provide a forum in which to review Care Plans and to agree and record decisions in consultation with all those who have a key interest in the child's life, in particular the child.

Independent Reviewing Officers (IROs) have been introduced to quality assure this process. They will chair all review meetings of looked after children, ensure the child is involved in the review and will challenge poor practice, and any drift in implementing the Care Plan. As a last resort the IRO will have power to refer a case to the Children and Family Court Advisory and Support Service (CAFCASS) which will be able to take the case to court if a child's human rights appear to be in breach.

3.17 We have to get the balance right between attempts at rehabilitation with the birth family and finding a permanent new home for the child in a timescale suited to them. The planning and review structure outlined in the box already provides the framework for securing this.

3.18 Permanence planning is not a matter of simply identifying the intended destination for a child. Services may be provided and placements used as part of an agreed plan to achieve permanence, without themselves representing permanence for the particular child.

3.19 The Government's goal is to ensure children benefit from high quality care planning by:

- encouraging early planning for permanence by local authorities and ensuring that all relevant placement options are considered. Concurrent planning may have a role here (see box below)

- ensuring that the different permanence options are equally credible, including long term fostering

- examining how access to support services affects a child's placement and permanence options

- extending the common assessment framework to cover the assessment of carers. Matching children with carers who can meet their assessed needs is a crucial part of delivering permanence plans.

Concurrent Planning

In **concurrent planning** the child is placed with approved foster carers who, as well as providing temporary care for the child, act as support to the birth parents in helping them meet the objectives of any rehabilitation plan. The carers are also approved as adopters so that if the rehabilitation plan is not successful the child does not need to move and can remain in the same placement while the adoption plan is developed and implemented.

Three projects in England that are currently using the concurrent planning model – the Goodman Project in Manchester, the Coram Family in London and Brighton & Hove – were the subject of an independent evaluation which found that the children involved had fewer moves and moved faster to a permanence option. Nearly all the placements were of single children aged under 12 months old. The authors of the evaluation concluded that "it is possible to say with confidence that concurrent planning worked well for the children in the study" [iii].

Supporting foster carers

3.20 Nearly 40,000 children are in foster care – that is almost two thirds of the total number of children in care[iv]. Foster carers play a unique and critical role in our communities, providing homes and care for particularly vulnerable children. This can range from providing a short break to a placement for a child with particular needs, to a family home for a child for many years. For children with more complex needs, therapeutic or intensive fostering may be an appropriate option.

3.21 Larger numbers of children, with increasingly complex needs, are coming into care and society is demanding more than ever before from foster carers. It is in this context that the Government needs to recruit and retain more foster carers.

3.22 To do this, we are seeking to provide foster carers with the training and support which they require to meet the needs of the children in their care. The National Minimum Standards for Fostering Services state clearly that fostering services must have a clear strategy for supporting carers, train foster carers so that they are able to provide high quality care, and provide foster carers with an allowance and agreed expenses which cover the full cost of caring for each child placed with them. Services are being inspected against these standards for the first time this year, and it is already clear that many services do not currently meet these standards.

3.23 The best agencies take a proactive approach to recruitment based on a clear strategy, earmarked resources and a targeted campaign, backed up through the provision of a large range of support services for foster carers. They will usually provide structured training linked to skills and a framework for continuing development. In some cases improved skills will be linked to higher fee payments. We want to see all fostering services achieve the results of the best and over time consider how payments for skills can contribute to retention and to the development of quality foster care placements.

3.24 In 2003-04 a £19.75 million Choice Protects grant has been allocated to local authorities to expand and strengthen their fostering services. Work is underway to establish a team of Choice Protects change agents to help local authorities improve the way they commission and provide services for looked after children. Additionally Choice Protects has commissioned a programme of work to help local authorities support foster carers and develop fostering services. These include good practice guidelines, research, and piloting innovative services such as treatment foster care for the most difficult to place children.

3.25 Through the Choice Protects programme the Government aims to improve the recruitment and retention of foster carers. The Government wants to build on this work programme further and is seeking views on radical and imaginative ways of encouraging people to become foster carers and ensuring that they are valued and recognised. This might involve:

- a national recruitment campaign

- encouraging more people to consider fostering, including groups such as single people, older people, unmarried couples and lone parents who may not realise they are eligible. Local partners, for example Jobcentre Plus, could play a part in making available information about fostering

- paid leave for foster carers and raising the statutory adoption pay to 90 percent of pay for the first six weeks of leave in line with statutory maternity pay, to help foster carers and adopters, where appropriate, to balance caring with their work. The Government is committed to commencing a review of the duty to consider requests for flexible working in 2006, and could consider these options at the same time:

  - a national award scheme to acknowledge the work of outstanding foster carers

  - a national helpline for foster carers, available 24 hours a day

  - support for foster carers subject to allegations similar to that currently provided for teachers

  - enhanced training opportunities and rewards for developing skills to care for children with particular difficulties

  - recognition and rewards for foster carers who support and mentor new foster carers

  - improved short break provision giving foster carers a break.

Residential Care

3.26 Currently approximately 7,750 children are placed in children homes, residential schools or other types of setting away from their families. Many of these children have challenging and complex needs. Young people placed in residential care are likely to be vulnerable teenagers.

3.27 A residential care placement by itself is unlikely to give a young person a secure sense of attachment but it may help secure a permanent placement. It can also be suitable for young people who are unable to live with their families but reject being fostered. All homes must meet National Minimum Standards and are inspected regularly.

3.28 Through the Choice Protects programme, guidance is being developed for publication in 2004. It will help local authorities to assess the needs of their population, improve commissioning and ensure better placements for children and young people who cannot live at home.

Adoption

3.29 The Government is currently implementing an extensive programme designed to modernise the adoption system. The aim of the programme is to increase the number of vulnerable children who benefit from a permanent family through adoption by:

- ensuring the child's needs are the paramount consideration in adoption

- recruiting more adopters and supporting them better

- improving local authorities' performance on adoption

- improving the efficiency and clarity of court processes.

3.30 Already this work has contributed to a significant increase in the number of looked after children who are adopted. In the year ending 31 March 2002, 3,400 looked after children were adopted, up 25 percent in just two years. To complete this important work, the Government will be:

- implementing the new approach to adoption set out in the Adoption and Children Act 2002

- monitoring and evaluating the implementation of the Adoption and Children Act 2002 and its wider adoption project.

Consultation Questions

Views are invited on the proposals set out in this Chapter. In particular:

- How can good quality decision-making by social services in relation to achieving permanence for the children for whom they are responsible best be achieved?

- Building on Choice Protects, what more can we do to recruit and retain more foster carers who are able to meet the needs of looked after children?

- How can local authorities, working with the voluntary, community and private sectors, develop a range of specialist parenting support services?

- Working with local authorities and other existing providers, what steps should the Government take to make home visiting services more widely available?

- What further action could be taken to extend the use of direct payments by families with disabled children?

- What more could be done to improve services for children and families of offenders?

---

i   DesForges C (2003) *The impact of parental involvement, parental support and family education on pupil achievement and adjustment.* (In draft for DfES.)

ii   This is the first of the Government's Objectives for Children's Social Services (*Modernising Social Services*, Department of Health, 1998)

iii   *The Role of Concurrent Planning: Making permanent placements for young children,* Monck et al, BAAF, 2003

iv   At 3 March 2002, 59,700 children were looked after, of whom 39,200 (66 percent) were in foster care.

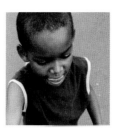

Early Intervention and Effective Protection

4

Victoria Climbié came into contact with several agencies, none of which acted on the warning signs. No one built up the full picture of her interactions with different services. Children with problems such as special educational needs, or behavioural disorders, or suffering from neglect, can also find that services often come too late. This Green Paper sets out the long term vision for how we intend to intervene earlier. It focuses on:

- **improving information sharing** between agencies, ensuring all local authorities have a list of children in their area, a list of the services they have had contact with, and the contact details of relevant professionals

- **establishing a common assessment framework.** The Government will move towards a common assessment framework across services for all children. The aim is for core

information to follow the child between services to reduce duplication

- **identifying lead professionals** to take the lead on each case where children are known to more than one specialist agency

- **integrating professionals** through multi-disciplinary teams responsible for identifying children at risk, and working with the child and family to ensure services are tailored to their needs

- **co-locating services** in and around schools, Sure Start Children's Centres, and primary care settings

- **ensuring effective child protection** procedures are in place across all organisations.

Improving information collection and sharing

4.1 The Victoria Climbié inquiry highlighted the failure to collect basic information and share it between agencies or across local authority boundaries. For instance, nobody checked whether Victoria was in school. Despite her case coming to the attention of various agencies on twelve occasions, professionals made decisions based on little information about Victoria's previous contact with a series of services. Judgements were made based on separate snapshots rather than a picture built up over time.

4.2 In many parts of the country, local authorities are developing innovative solutions to information sharing. In some areas, these are based on the use of technology to enable professionals to register early concerns about a child's needs, as in Telford and Wrekin's AWARE project, and through the Connexions Customer Information System.

4.3 The long term aim is to build on these developments to integrate information across services and ensure professionals share concerns at an early stage. To achieve this, we want to see a local information hub

Telford and Wrekin's AWARE system brings together data from existing databases from schools, other education services, the youth offending service, social care, primary care trust and family protection unit and extracts and improves the quality of non-sensitive data. Information on the child's name, address, gender, date of birth, and siblings and which agencies and practitioners the child is involved with is readily and securely available to practitioners. But to protect confidentiality unnecessary case details are not given out. The NHS number is used as a personal identifier.

Using the latest technologies AWARE provides practitioners from all agencies with a number of facilities to assist them in preventative work, and more integrated provision of services:

● level of concerns can be placed by practitioners against a child, which generate 'traffic light' markers allowing the level of concern to be shared across agencies, patterns to be identified , and so on

● practitioners are provided with a secure messaging facility between agencies

● a 'who's who' of all practitioners makes contacting them easier

● a document library enables all practitioners to access common documents and procedures

developed in every authority consisting of a list of all the children living in their area and basic details including:

- name, address and date of birth
- school attended or if excluded or refused access
- GP
- a flag stating whether the child is known to agencies such as education welfare, social services, police and Youth Offending Teams (YOTs), and if so, the contact details of the professional dealing with the case
- where a child is known to more than one specialist agency, the lead professional who takes overall responsibility for the case.

The information hub

4.4 An agency coming into contact with a child would be able to check this list of information before deciding how best to proceed. The long term vision is that information is stored and accessed electronically by a range of agencies.

Such information systems will be based on national data standards to enable the exchange of information between local authorities and partner agencies, and capable of interaction with other data sets.

4.5 In order to capture fully the concerns of a range of professionals over time, there is a strong case for giving practitioners the ability to flag on the system early warnings when they have a concern about a child which in itself may not be a trigger or meet the usual thresholds for intervention. The decision to place such a flag of concern on a child's record, which could be picked up by another agency making a similar judgement, lies with the practitioners.

4.6 It would be a matter of professional judgement whether the combination of two or more flags of minor concern warranted some form of action. A framework for exercising this judgement should be developed and agreed by local agencies. There is a balance to strike between sharing enough information to help safeguard children effectively and preserving

Figure 1

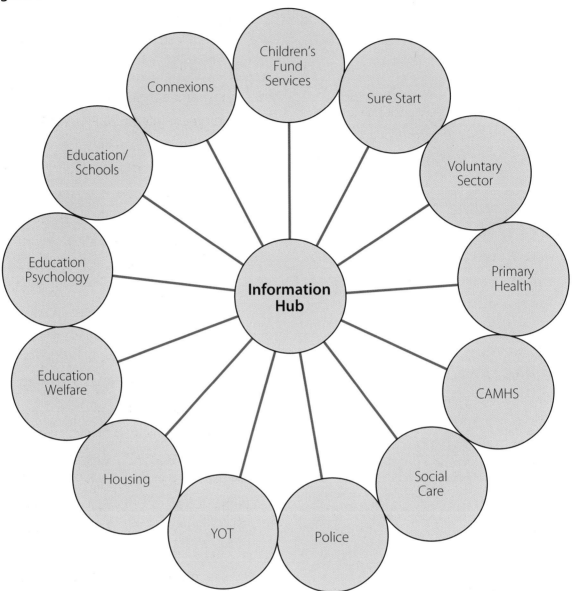

individuals' privacy. The Government wants to prevent situations where a child does not receive the help they need because of too rigid an interpretation of the privacy of the child and their family. In order to get the balance right, we are consulting on the circumstances (in addition to child protection and youth offending) under which information about a child could or must be shared, for preventative purposes, without the consent of the child or their carers. We would also welcome views on whether warning signs should reflect factors within the family such as imprisonment, domestic violence, mental health or substance misuse problems amongst parents and carers.

4.7 Systems would hold records for every child or young person resident in a local authority area. This would be important in enabling practitioners to ensure that no children or young people are overlooked. Information would be updated by practitioners in response to changes in the child's life. Local protocols would be in place, reflecting national standards to ensure this happened. Some of the changes would be made directly to the system. Other updates would be generated by standard alerts and events originating from local case management systems, but in strict accordance with the national framework to ensure reliable data transfer. For example, a child without a current educational record in the system should generate an alert. National standards would be in place to ensure reliable and secure exchange of data between local authorities, including upper and lower tier authorities.

Getting there

4.8 To take forward such information sharing systems, the Government is:

- providing up to £1 million to 10 'Identification, Referral and Tracking' (IRT) trailblazers involving 15 local authorities to test out approaches. We are putting in place a central team to learn lessons and develop a national framework for local information sharing systems. We will have early lessons from the trailblazers by December 2003, and more detailed information by late summer 2004. By the end of 2004, we aim to set out how the lessons from the trailblazers can be reflected across the country. As part of this, the Government will examine the potential benefits and risks of introducing

ICT-based information sharing systems and whether it is feasible to overcome the considerable technical challenges in this area

- removing the legal barriers. The Government intends to legislate at the first opportunity to enable information sharing to happen at an earlier stage to prevent problems escalating. In anticipation of legislative change, in August 2003 we issued guidance[i] on how to apply current legislation. The law provides safeguards for individuals but it does not prevent joint working. Information can be shared quickly and efficiently whenever it is necessary and appropriate to do so. We expect local authorities and their partners to take the lead in establishing local information sharing arrangements. The guidance seeks to enable all professionals working with children to develop a common understanding of the legal framework to ensure that information is properly shared so that children can be protected. It also provides best practice examples of protocols and agreements that are already in place in authorities across the country

- removing the technical barriers. To ensure that different electronic systems are able to exchange information about a particular child securely and accurately across local authority boundaries, the Government plans to announce, by the end of 2003, how it will define a single identifying number to support electronic information transfer. This could build on the use of existing identifiers such as the NHS number or the National Insurance number. In addition, as part of the national framework, the Government will set out common data standards on the recording of information so that data can be transferred easily between agencies

- removing the organisational boundaries. The proposals set out in Chapter Five are aimed at improving integration across services, which should make information sharing easier. The Government expects local authorities and their partners to develop and agree clear information sharing protocols, which are communicated actively to frontline workers in all agencies

- removing professional and cultural barriers. Technical solutions alone will not secure the changes that the Government is seeking to achieve. Reforming professional cultures is as important as the development of any technical systems. For local authorities, the immediate aim is to facilitate an effective dialogue between professionals from the various services and organisations working with children. Information sharing should be an important element in the common training for professionals who come into contact with children. As part of the move towards integrated structures, set out in Chapter Five, it will be important for local authorities to lead a process of cultural change which includes information sharing and

developing a common understanding of terms across services. Recent guidance, *What To Do If You're Worried A Child Is Being Abused*, made it clear that professionals must consider the risk of not sharing information about children with other professionals, alongside concerns about respecting a child or family's right to privacy.

Immediate action

4.9 The Government is providing £100,000 to each unitary and county council in the current year to help them develop better information sharing between professionals. Authorities will be expected to have appointed a project manager or other named individual with specific responsibility for IRT project development and implementation.

4.10 By the autumn, authorities are expected to have carried out an audit of existing local service provision and practice. This audit should identify platforms for the further development of information sharing arrangements and also highlight gaps and duplication. Local authorities and their partners should build on the work already being undertaken by different agencies, in particular, the Connexions Customer Information System being rolled out in March 2004, and the Integrated Children's System, due to be implemented by the end of 2005.

4.11 The recent guidance sets out a detailed timetable for action by local authorities on information sharing. Further details are set out in an Appendix to this document. The project manager will take responsibility for developing the minimum requirements and, in the longer term, they could be in charge of developing a list of children in the area, ensuring that paper or electronic filing systems enable practitioners to know which children are known to multiple services, or pursuing cases where children enter or leave their area.

4.12 Technical developments are only part of the picture. The Government is keen to ensure information can be shared more effectively in advance of technical developments. As part of this, we would be interested in views on how to ensure effective transfer of information across boundaries. For instance, it will be important to ensure effective procedures so that housing departments, which may be the first service to identify a family moving between or within local authority areas, work effectively with education, social services and other agencies to ensure service delivery is seamless.

Common assessment framework

4.13 Children may receive many assessments during their childhood. Health visiting teams make assessments of health and development in early childhood. All children receive a baseline assessment in the first year of primary school and secondary schools are increasingly introducing individual learning plans. Children who are referred to other services also receive assessments from social services,

Connexions, Youth Offending Teams, education psychologists and others.

4.14 Reform is needed to tackle two weaknesses:

● children with multiple needs may be subject to multiple assessments by different people, each collecting similar information but using different professional terms and categories. The core information does not follow the child. This is not only an inefficient use of resources, but also alienating for the child and family who have to tell the same story to several professionals but may receive little practical help as a result

● some frontline services, such as the police, schools and health, may refer children to social services without a preliminary assessment of the child's needs. As a result, social services may be overwhelmed with inappropriate cases, and children and families may undergo initial assessments unnecessarily. Frontline professionals such as pastoral staff in schools, who may already have trusting relationships with the child or parent, may be in a better position to discuss initial concerns with a child or parent, and work with them over time, than a social worker with whom the family has had no previous contact.

4.15 In several areas, services have developed effective ways of combatting these challenges through a common assessment framework, as in North Lincolnshire.

The **North Lincolnshire Common Assessment** is used by any professional coming into contact with a child. The aim is for all services to take responsibility for identifying children's needs before referring vague concerns or value based judgements to other services.

The simple assessment has been designed to be completed in around one hour. Many teachers and other school staff find the assessment a useful tool to identify the real needs of a child about whom they are concerned. Rather than purely arranging specialist educational support for a child who is struggling at school, the assessment identifies all the child's needs, not just the educational ones, which may require intervention. The views of the parent/carer and the child are sought where appropriate.

The advantages of using a common assessment framework across agencies are:

- referrals are appropriate. During the pilot phase, child concern referrals to social services dropped by 64 percent – in many cases this was due to other agencies taking responsibility for addressing the child's needs themselves. Previously, the police made 50-60 referrals to social services per month. Now the figure is 8-9. This means social services provide more services rather than simply dealing with unnecessary referrals

- children and families do not have to repeat their information to different professionals as the assessment process is the same, irrespective of which agency the child and family go to for help

- services are provided more promptly and coherently as professionals trust one another's assessment of need as it has been made using agreed 'common' indicators of need about what is required by a child and their family

- assessments are triggered when a concern about a child is raised, rather than when the child reaches a crisis point

- if any further assessments are required, these then build upon the Common Assessment, rather than duplicate it.

4.16 To develop this approach further, the Government will lead work to develop a common assessment framework. This will draw on the current framework for the assessment of children in need and their families, which is used by social services; the Connexions Assessment, Planning, Implementation and Review System; the

Youth Justice Board's Asset tool; the SEN code of practice; and assessments conducted by health visitors. It will look at the extent to which the North Lincolnshire model of assessments can be rolled out, with responsibility being more firmly embedded in universal services. It will also look at how children can be an active part of the assessment process, and how assessment can identify strengths and opportunities as well as needs and risks. In the light of views expressed during the consultation period, the Government will set up a team to draw up and develop a common assessment framework by March 2004 with a view to introduction by September 2004.

4.17 As well as reducing unnecessary assessment, the process of developing and using a common assessment framework will have a critical role to play in the drive to improve inter-professional relationships. It will underpin and be reinforced by the structural and workforce reforms set out in Chapters Five and Six.

Lead professional

4.18 Children may be in contact with more than one specialist service at a time. For instance, a child may be truanting, offending, and suffering from abuse at home, and may have special educational needs. As a result, children can receive services that risk duplicating or cutting across each other.

4.19 The creation of Connexions was designed to ensure that, for those aged 13-19, there is a single professional co-ordinating services for the individual, providing some continuity over time to develop trust. Behaviour and Education Support Teams, learning mentors, and activities funded by the Children's Fund also involve developing a 'key worker' to co-ordinate support. In social services, a key worker is allocated to children on the child protection register and looked after children.

By pooling resources with Connexions, Liverpool leaving care service has nearly doubled the number of its young people entering employment, training or education. In 1999 **30% of 18 year old care leavers** were either in jobs, studying or training for qualifications. By September 2002 this had risen to **nearly 57%.**

The CLICS project is a partnership between Liverpool leaving care service and Connexions with three Connexions Personal Advisers working as part of the Leaving care team. Working together, the project ensures contact is maintained with young people and helps to put in place tailored training and learning opportunities.

4.20 The Government would welcome views on how to improve case management more widely than through these sorts of targeted programmes. As a basic minimum, we would like to ensure that where a child is known to more than one specialist service, there is a designated 'lead professional' who would co-ordinate service provision. The lead professional would provide the basis for the development of much more effective information sharing to support service delivery.

4.21 For most children, the lead professional role may be best fulfilled by someone from the service that has the most contact with the child day to day (school based staff from school age, Connexions personal advisers from age 13-19, and social workers for looked after children). For a child with complex needs, a more specialist service might host the lead professional role. Family circumstances would dictate whether it is more appropriate for siblings to have the same or a different key worker.

4.22 The lead professional could also act as the 'gatekeeper' for information sharing systems highlighted above. Other professionals could have partial access but only the lead professional would be aware of the detail. It could be the lead professional who would make a judgement about whether, taken together, the early warnings logged by different practitioners merited intervention.

Multi-disciplinary teams

4.23 Common assessments and information sharing will be a major step forward but further integration is also needed. Children could still be faced with a series of different professionals who work in different offices to different managers, rather than one trusted adult providing continuity of support. Referrals between agencies could still lead to misunderstandings and delays.

4.24 These more fundamental challenges need to be addressed through different ways of working, which integrate education, social care and health services around the needs of children rather than providers. Based on current best practice such as that developed in Youth Offending Teams, the goal is to move towards multi-disciplinary teams that bring together the relevant professionals who can work together in places easily accessible to children and families.

4.25 Professionals and para-professionals will increasingly work alongside each other in the same teams. Teams must have a structure which enables professionals within them to have both continuous professional development and the appropriate clinical and professional governance, with clear lines of professional accountability. This should ensure that multi-disciplinary teams are able to benefit from a wide range of professionals working together, without losing the advantages of those professionals' individual specialisms.

The Multi Agency Preventative (MAP) Project, Tower Hamlets addresses emotional and behavioural problems amongst Bangladeshi pupils in secondary schools, targeting particularly those at risk of becoming aggressive, disaffected, isolated or depressed, and girls at risk of self-harming. The project is a joint intervention between health, social services, education and the voluntary sector, and employs a range of staff including clinical psychologists, youth workers, community resource officers and social workers. The project offers solution-focused counselling, school based therapeutic support groups, and optional recreational activities including residential programmes during school holidays, aimed at raising the young person's self-esteem. Various awareness raising initiatives are taken to involve, educate and inform parents and carers and members of the Bangladeshi community about meeting the needs of children at risk of emotional and behavioural problems.

Manchester BEST. Manchester LEA has used funding from the Behaviour Improvement Programme (BIP) to establish four multi-agency Behaviour and Education Support Teams (BESTs) to work across clusters of schools consisting of a target secondary school and its main associated primaries where there are high numbers of children with emotional and behavioural needs.

One such cluster includes **Ducie High School,** where the team is located in the school, providing easy access to a range of specialist services. The team at Ducie encompasses an education welfare officer, a family intervention worker from social services, an educational psychologist, a play worker (brought in specifically to address a problem with behaviour during playtimes), and two behaviour support workers. Through the BIP in Manchester, CAMHS offers support (and training) to schools. Protocols are in place so that BIP pupils can access specialist mental health services when needed. The team operates on a number of levels, supporting not only the needs of individual pupils and their families, but also the wider school community through group intervention work, staff training and surgeries, and emotional literacy programmes. Family work is a strong feature of Manchester BESTs. Early indications show that the team has already had an impact in terms of faster successful case closures. There have also been improvements in exclusion, attendance and crime figures.

4.26 Over time, professionals and non-professionals might increasingly work together in different types of teams, involving some or all of:

- health visitors
- GPs
- social workers
- education welfare officers
- youth and community workers
- Connexions personal advisers
- education psychologists
- children's mental health professionals
- speech and language therapists and other allied health professionals
- young people's substance misuse workers
- learning mentors and school support staff
- school nurses
- home visitors, volunteers and mentors
- statutory and voluntary homelessness agencies

4.27 The multi-disciplinary teams would use the common assessment framework

described earlier. They would be responsible for ensuring children's needs are met effectively. This would involve:

- identifying children at risk, or receiving referrals and self-referrals
- contacting and engaging children and their families and gaining their trust
- working with the child and family to develop an individual action plan setting out the key goals agreed with the child and the parents, and the resources that would be harnessed to support these goals
- either providing services from within the team or brokering support from mainstream and specialist services

Co-location around schools, Sure Start Children's Centres, and primary care

4.28 There is a strong case for basing multi-disciplinary teams in and around the places where many children spend much of their time, such as schools and Sure Start Children's Centres, and also primary care centres. This would promote self-referral into services and enable children's social workers and other professionals to engage in dialogue with teaching and school support

The benefits of co-location. Mayday University Hospital, Croydon, has two children's social services teams on site, providing a comprehensive assessment social work function for children and their families who are resident in Croydon and are receiving as inpatients or outpatients services from the hospital, and a proactive liaison/assessment role with other authorities for children who are inpatients at the hospital.

staff. Embedding targeted services within universal settings can ensure more rapid support without the delay of formal referral, and enable frontline professionals to seek help and advice. Developing networks across universal and specialist professionals can strengthen inter-professional relationships and trust.

4.29 Co-location requires considerable local flexibility as the opportunities and barriers differ depending on local geography. While a shift towards more school based services is sensible, other settings, such as neighbourhood based services, will still be important, particularly in re-engaging young people who have left school at 16 and are not in education or training.

4.30 The previous Chapter noted how clusters of schools can work together to:

- deploy multi-disciplinary teams collectively, to assess and address needs, for example providing advice and support on special educational needs, and being able to refer on to more specialist services where necessary

- help retain within the school system children who might otherwise be excluded, or help reintegrate children and young people who have been outside the school system

- provide pastoral support to all children, with key worker support to those needing a range of services such as disabled children

- provide access to personal development opportunities, including through partnership with statutory and voluntary youth services and Connexions.

4.31 It would be possible to develop from the current model in which multi-agency teams support a cluster of schools, as in the Behaviour Improvement Programme, to one in which a cluster of schools and education institutions including pupil referral units, early years' settings, Sure Start, further education colleges and Connexions, might choose to take responsibility for offering multi-disciplinary services to all children in their area. With appropriate administrative and management support, such arrangements might better meet the full range of children's needs. Focusing on a particular area or cluster of settings can ensure services are more rooted in a community, particularly if, as in Sure Start local programmes, the governance arrangements encourage community involvement.

4.32 The Government would also be interested in how such multi-disciplinary teams can make better use of information to prioritise particular groups of children. For instance, they could ensure that children who are truanting or are living in temporary accommodation and known to social services have an effective package of support, or potentially focus on the children not achieving expected results at key stages. Effective targeting can be supported not only by formal data but also informal relationships with professionals and the local community.

Effective protection

4.33 The Victoria Climbié Inquiry and the Joint Chief Inspectors' reports on safeguarding children identified a number of problems with the current system for safeguarding children. They also showed how to move towards a better children's safeguards system, where child protection services are not separate from support for families, but are part of the spectrum of services provided to help and support children and families.

4.34 The Government has already begun to take action. In May 2003, we issued a booklet called *What To Do If You're Worried A Child Is Being Abused*. This booklet is designed to help people to protect children more effectively.

4.35 The Government is publishing alongside this Green Paper its detailed response to the Victoria Climbié Inquiry Report and the Joint Chief Inspectors' report on safeguarding services. The Victoria Climbié Inquiry Report made clear that the statutory framework covering child protection is sound but work was needed to ensure this was effectively delivered. The next Chapters set out how the barriers to implementing effective child protection procedures will be addressed through:

- clear practice standards across services, setting out what should be done in relation to child protection

- shared responsibility across all agencies for protecting children through new statutory duties

- someone in charge locally with statutory responsibilities for child protection and co-ordinating the work of social services, police, housing, education, and other key services

- an inspection system that assesses how well agencies work together to create an effective system of protection

- workforce reform to ensure all people working with children are trained in child protection.

4.36 These changes will tackle the long term weaknesses in the system. However, the response document sets out the immediate steps the Government is taking in:

- revising and shortening the existing range of Children Act 1989 Regulations and Guidance

- auditing safeguarding children activity of local authorities with social services responsibilities, NHS bodies and police forces

- raising the priority of safeguarding children amongst all relevant agencies/organisations.

Consultation Questions

Views are invited on the information sharing proposals set out in this Chapter. In particular:

- What currently gets in the way of effective information sharing, and how can we remove the barriers?

- What should be the thresholds and triggers for sharing information about a child?

- What are the circumstances (in addition to child protection and youth offending) under which information about a child could or must be shared without the consent of the child or their carers?

- Should information on parents and carers, such as domestic violence, imprisonment, mental health or drug problems, be shared?

- How can we ensure that no children slip through the system?

- What issues might stand in the way of effective information transfer across local authority boundaries?

- Should a unique identifying number be used?

- Views are also invited on the proposals relating to multi-disciplinary teams:

  - What are the barriers to developing them further in a range of settings?

  - How can we ensure multi-disciplinary teams have greater leverage over mainstream and specialist services?

i   IRT: Guidance on Information Sharing can be found online at http://www.dfes.gov.uk/publications/keys.html.

Accountability and Integration – Locally, Regionally and Nationally

The Government's aim is that there should be one person in charge locally and nationally with the responsibility for improving children's lives. Key services for children should be integrated within a single organisational focus at both levels. To achieve this the Government will:

- legislate to create the post of **Director of Children's Services**, accountable for local authority education and children's social services

- legislate to create **a lead council member for children**

- in the long term, integrate key services for children and young people under the Director of Children's Services as part of Children's Trusts. These bring together local authority education and children's social services, some children's health services, Connexions, and can include other services such as Youth Offending Teams. Children's Trusts will normally be part of the local authority and will report to local elected members

- require local authorities to work closely with public, private and voluntary organisations to improve outcomes for children. Local authorities will be given flexibility over how this partnership working is undertaken

- in relation to child protection, require the creation of **Local Safeguarding Children Boards** as the statutory successors to Area Child Protection Committees.

To support local integration, the Government has created a new **Minister for Children, Young People and Families** in the Department for Education and

Skills to co-ordinate policies across Government.

The Government will encourage joining up locally by:

- ensuring children are a priority across services. Local bodies such as the police and health organisations will, subject to consultation, have a new duty to safeguard children, promote their well-being and work together through these partnership arrangements. We also intend to give local authorities a duty to promote the educational achievement of children in care

- setting out clear practice standards expected of each agency in relation to children

- rationalising performance targets, plans, funding streams, financial accountability and indicators

- creating an integrated **inspection framework for children's services.** Ofsted will take the lead in bringing together joint inspection teams. This will ensure services are judged on how well they work together

- creating an **improvement and intervention function** to drive up performance by sharing effective practice, and intervening where services are failing.

Real service improvement is only attainable through involving children and young people and listening to their views. This Chapter sets out proposals for a new **Children's Commissioner** to act as an independent champion.

The case for change

Local fragmentation

5.1 Children's needs are complex and rarely fit neatly within one set of organisational boundaries. For instance, a child with behavioural problems due to parental neglect may be considered a child with special educational needs by the LEA, a 'child in need' by social services, or having a 'conduct disorder' by a child and adolescent mental health team. If the child truants, they may come into contact with the education welfare service, and if they offend they will come into contact with the police and the Youth Offending Team. The categories around which services are organised are overlapping, fluid and, in some cases, blurred.

5.2 The fragmentation of responsibilities for children leads to problems such as:

- information not being shared between agencies and concerns not being passed on. As a result children may slip through the net or receive services only when problems become severe

- a child may receive assessments from different agencies which duplicate rather than complement each other

- several professionals may be in contact with a child over time but no single person provides continuity or co-ordinates services

- several agencies spend some money on the child rather than one agency spending an appropriate amount on a co-ordinated package of support

- services may disagree about whether the child falls into their categories and may try to pass on difficult cases to other organisations

- professionals and services may be based in different locations rather than co-located. Co-location can make services more accessible to users, improve inter-professional relationships and ways of working

- services are planned and commissioned to focus on one particular objective – such as childcare, truancy, or family abuse. Planning services in the round can enable a better response to support the child and better value for money. Joint commissioning can enable the creation of services that deliver multiple dividends such as Children's Centres and extended schools.

5.3 In this country, and internationally, new institutional arrangements are emerging that break down existing organisational boundaries. For instance, some local authorities, such as Hertfordshire, Wiltshire, and Brighton & Hove have merged children's social services and education to form children, schools and families departments. In other countries, institutions that integrate services around the child are also emerging, such as Children and Families Services

Authorities in Canada, and the Family and Community Trust in Missouri.

National fragmentation

5.4 An underlying cause of local fragmentation is conflicting messages and incentives at national level. Organisations are exhorted to work together but the targets, plans and inspection regimes focus on how institutions work in isolation.

5.5 This analysis is not new. It accords with the messages set out in *Serving Children Well*, which was published jointly by the Local Government Association (LGA), Association of Directors of Social Services (ADSS), Association of Chief Education Officers (ACEO), Confed and the NHS Confederation. It also fits with the analysis in the Victoria Climbié Inquiry Report. However, while the problem has long been recognised, the scale of the problem has historically not been matched by proportionate solutions.

Vision

5.6 We want to move to a system locally and nationally where there is:

- clear overall accountability for services for children, young people and families

- integration of key services around the needs of children, in particular, education, social care, health, youth justice, and Connexions.

5.7 To achieve better outcomes for children and young people, the Government wants to move to a system where the key services and budgets for children and young people are placed within a single organisational focus locally. As a first step, the Government is committed to tackling the critical boundary between children's social services and education. The majority of spending on children's services by local authorities is within these two departments. Improving key outcomes such as the education of children in care, or life chances for disabled children, is particularly dependent on integration across education and social services.

5.8 The Government intends to legislate at the next available opportunity to require all local authorities to appoint a **Director of Children's Services**. The Director would be accountable for education and social services and for overseeing services for children delegated to the local authority by other services. The current legislation requiring the appointment of a Chief Education Officer and a Director of Social Services will be amended to reflect this. We expect that in time this will lead to a single Children's Department in most authorities, although we will not require it. Councils will still be required to ensure accountability arrangements are in place for social services functions for adults.

5.9 In legislating to require the appointment of a Director of Children's Services, the Government will ensure that there is sufficient flexibility for all local authorities to make this change in a way which fits their local circumstances, minimises disruption and maintains service standards.

5.10 Legislation will enable authorities to make such appointments straight away, and will require that they all do so in due course. Authorities will be expected to set up clear transitional arrangements which secure as soon as possible an appropriate single point of accountability for children's services. This may involve those who currently have the role of, for example, Chief Executive or current Chief Education Officers or Directors of Social Services. The responsibilities of the Director of Children's Services must include children's social services and education but need not be limited to these services: the Director may also be responsible, for example, for housing or leisure services. The key is that there should be one person in charge of children's services and clarity at all times as to who that person is. We also intend to legislate to introduce a duty on local authorities to promote the educational achievement of children in care. This duty could be exercised through the Director of Children's Services.

5.11 In addition to clearer accountability at official level, the Government will also legislate to create a **lead council member for children**.

5.12 The Government's long term vision is to integrate key services within a single organisational focus. The preferred model for achieving this integration is **Children's Trusts**. Most areas should have Trusts by 2006.

5.13 Children's Trusts go beyond children, families and schools departments by including children's health services (through

Section 31 of the Health Act 1999). Trusts may also include other services such as Connexions and Youth Offending Teams. Children's Trusts will normally sit within the local authority and report to the Director of Children's Services who will report through the Chief Executive to elected members.

5.14 The key services that should be within the Trust are:

- local education authority – potentially all education functions, including the education welfare service, youth service, special educational needs and educational psychology, childcare and early years education, and school improvement

- children's social services – including assessment and services for children in need such as family support, foster and residential care, adoption services, childcare, advocacy services and child protection, and services for care leavers

- Community and acute health services – such as community paediatrics, services commissioned by Drug Action Teams, teenage pregnancy co-ordinators, and locally commissioned and provided Child and Adolescent Mental Health Services. They could also include speech and language therapy, health visiting and occupational therapy services concerned with children and families. Primary Care Trusts will be able to delegate functions into the Children's Trust, and will be able to pool funds with the local authority.

Other services which may be part of the Trust include:

- **Youth Offending Teams** – multi-disciplinary teams working with young people and their families to prevent offending

- **Connexions Service** – multi-agency information, advice and guidance service for 13-19s.

5.15 Children's Trusts will commission services and may provide them directly or contract with public, private or voluntary sector organisations. Staff providing the services may be seconded into the Trust or transferred.

Sheffield Children's Trust

The Sheffield Children's Trust will be a whole systems approach – to commission and provide services to all 0-19 year olds in the city. Partners will share aims, objectives and key indicators, which focus the Trust on children and their families. The Trust will include Connexions, leisure and housing in the partnership. A common assessment process has already been developed and agreed. There are mechanisms to involve children and families in the development of services. The Sheffield Children's Trust will develop extended schools and many services will be delivered around these schools.

What will be the key features of Children's Trusts?

5.16 Children's Trusts will have the following core features:

- clear short and long term objectives covering the five Green Paper outcome areas of: enjoying and achieving, staying safe, being healthy, making a positive contribution, and economic well-being

- a Director of Children's Services in overall charge of delivering these outcomes and responsible for services within the Trust and co-ordination of services outside the organisation

- a single planning and commissioning function supported by pooled budgets. This would involve developing an overall picture of children's needs within an area, and developing provision through public, private, voluntary and community providers to respond to those needs. The Trust should involve children and families in putting together the picture of their needs and in designing the services to meet those needs. It would also involve developing arrangements for pooled budgets through a Section 31 agreement.

5.17 The integration of objectives, planning and commissioning through Children's Trusts is designed to achieve the integration of frontline service provision as outlined in the previous Chapter. This is expected to include:

- co-located services such as Children's Centres and extended schools

- multi-disciplinary teams and a key worker system

- a common assessment framework across services

- information sharing systems across services so that warning signs are aggregated, and children's outcomes are measured over time

- joint training with some identical modules so that staff have a single message about key policies and procedures such as a child protection and can learn about each other's roles and responsibilities

- effective arrangements for safeguarding children

- arrangements for addressing interface issues with other services, such as services for parents with mental health problems.

5.18 The move to Children's Trusts is an ambitious agenda. The pace of change will need to vary according to local circumstances, particularly given that health services and Connexions Partnerships are often not coterminous with local authorities, which could add to the complexity of the transition. It will be essential to manage change so that standards of practice and care are not disrupted.

5.19 As set out above, the Government expects localities to develop a change programme for implementing the framework set out in the Green Paper. As a minimum, PCTs will be asked to ensure that the relevant sections of their delivery plans in relation to children are agreed with the Director of Children's Services. Delegation of commissioning and the transfer of budgets is the preferred model. Partnership working on children's services is an integral part of the agreement that PCTs reach with Strategic Health Authorities as part of the performance management system.

5.20 The Government is also keen to see a closer integration of the services provided by education welfare services, Children's Fund, Connexions, Youth Service, learning mentors, and Behaviour and Education Support Teams. The total resource going into these services is over £1 billion.

5.21 The Government wants Connexions to play a full part in Children's Trusts. To reinforce this, the Government will, through Connexions business planning guidance from 2005:

- ask Connexions Partnerships to use Children's Trusts, where appropriate, as their local management committees. This will give Trusts an influence over the use of resource for the local authority area. The amount of Connexions resource for each local authority area should be clearly identified by the Partnership

- expect that Connexions business plans should be signed off by local Children's Trusts before Ministers will agree them. However, because of the way that Connexions is administered, the Connexions Partnership Chief Executive will have the final say in the plan that is submitted and Ministers would have

discretion to sign off plans without agreement by Children's Trusts to avoid disputes blocking the delivery of Connexions.

How Children's Trusts will relate to other organisations

5.22 Children's Trusts will integrate the functions of many key organisations that come into contact with children, young people and families. But some public sector organisations will remain outside the Trust, such as the police, the Learning and Skills Council, some health functions, and housing departments. Trusts will need to develop close relationships with a network of private, voluntary and community sector organisations.

5.23 The Government intends to legislate to ensure co-operation between local authorities and other public, private and voluntary organisations to improve outcomes for children. We intend to allow flexibility over how this partnership working is undertaken. In many areas, this may involve building on the existing Children and Young People's Strategic Partnerships.

Local Safeguarding Children Boards

5.24 One area that requires wider partnership than Children's Trusts is the safeguarding of children. This is currently managed through Area Child Protection Committees (ACPCs). The Joint Chief Inspectors' report *Safeguarding Children* notes that these arrangements are not working well in some areas. This has been because of the low priority given to safeguarding children by some of the bodies involved. This can manifest itself in lack of resources for child protection and lack of senior management commitment. ACPCs have often had limited influence on strategic planning and the allocation of resources.

5.25 The Government therefore intends to legislate to ensure that local authorities have a duty to set up Local Safeguarding Children Boards consisting of representatives from the partner agencies, including housing, health, police and probation services. Local Safeguarding Children Boards will co-ordinate the functions of all partner agencies in relation to safeguarding children. These boards will replace current ACPCs and we expect that they will be chaired by the Director of Children's Services.

5.26 The role of the Local Safeguarding Children Boards might include agreeing the contribution each agency will make to achieving the joint aim of safeguarding children and deciding how any pooled funds should be allocated. Local Safeguarding Children Boards may have responsibility for current ACPC responsibilities as set out in *Working Together to Safeguard Children* (1999). In addition they could commission independent serious case reviews, and manage a service to look at unexpected child deaths to decide which need serious case reviews, and draw out any public health lessons.

Regional arrangements

5.27 Government Offices for the Regions represent Government in the regions. They represent ten Departments and work to deliver central policies in a way that is responsive to local communities. Government Offices already support programmes for children and young people, for example, neighbourhood renewal, Connexions, Sure Start and Children's Fund. Government Offices co-ordinate this work through Children's Groups (GOCG), bringing together the various interests and activities that support delivery on the ground to ensure coherence. We will examine how central Government can use regional arrangements to support more effectively the delivery of services for children and families.

National arrangements

5.28 Key causes of fragmentation locally are separate targets, planning requirements, funding streams, and inspection systems nationally. Where localities attempt to join up services – for instance across the local education authority and children's social services – central Government still expects them to account for money separately, and separate inspectorates assess them, even if operationally services are integrated, and outcomes mutually reinforcing.

5.29 The Government is committed to supporting integration locally and encouraging all services to give priority to safeguarding children. A start has been made in this direction through the move towards joint inspections, but more needs to be done.

5.30 The Government has announced the integration of national policy for children and young people within the Department for Education and Skills, with a new Minister for Children, Young People and Families. These changes bring together policy on children's social services, teenage pregnancy, family and parenting law and support, and family policy with education. By putting children's services together within a single department and strengthening co-ordination arrangements across Government, the Government is putting children at the heart of policy development and service delivery and ensuring better integration. The Minister will work with a board of stakeholders, including local government and the voluntary sector, to improve the delivery and cohesiveness of Government policy on children and young people.

5.31 This single focus will ensure integrated policy development and unified national leadership to develop:

- a standard setting mechanism within the Department for Education and Skills, charged with removing barriers to effectiveness and reducing the bureaucratic burden of overlapping planning requirements, standards and guidance

- an integrated inspection framework and lead inspectorate for children to ensure services are judged on how well they work together

- an intervention and improvement mechanism to drive up performance everywhere, and intervene in areas where national standards are not being met.

Standard setting

5.32 The Government intends to create a standard setting mechanism that would set out the outcomes and practice standards expected of localities. This will build on the standards for health and social care that will be set out in the National Service Framework for Children to be published next year. The standard setting mechanism should set out what is expected of different agencies in terms of contributing to children's outcomes, including child protection. This function will need to work with Departments across Whitehall to simplify the performance management system for children's services. This will involve:

- rationalisation of targets to create fewer targets that are more complementary across services and are focused on core outcomes

- streamlining planning requirements, building on reforms already undertaken such as the creation of a single Education Plan for LEAs by April 2006

- rationalisation of the number of funding streams for children's services through the next Spending Review process

- ensuring national guidance on service standards is clear.

5.33 The Government will continue to work with others to ensure child protection is a priority across agencies including the police and health services. The Government has brought safeguarding within the framework of clinical governance through the new

National Service Framework hospital standard, following the recommendations of Lord Laming. Child protection is included in the National Policing Plan. This plan is currently under review and the new plan will be published in November 2003.

5.34 The Government has already introduced a new duty under the Education Act 2002 on local education authorities, schools and further education institutions to underpin and reinforce the priority given to safeguarding and protecting children. Under the Act, LEAs and the governing bodies of schools and FE institutions will be required to make arrangements to carry out their functions with a view to safeguarding and promoting the welfare of children, and to have regard to guidance issued by the Secretary of State in drawing up those arrangements. The new duty will come into force on 1 April 2004. DfES will issue new guidance to assist with implementation.

5.35 In addition, we intend, subject to consultation, to place a duty on all relevant local bodies (e.g. such as the police and health organisations) in exercising their normal functions, to have regard to safeguarding children, promoting their well-being and working together through the local partnership arrangements.

Inspection

5.36 The Government is committed to ensuring inspection captures how well services work together to improve children's lives within a framework that is consistent with the recommendations of the recent Office for Public Services Reform review. To do this, we intend to create an integrated inspection framework across children's services. Ofsted will take the lead in developing a framework for integrated inspections in consultation with Commission for Social Care Improvement, Commission for Health Improvement (CHI) and the Audit Commission. Where appropriate, they will bring together joint teams to carry out area-based inspections of education, social services, Connexions, youth services and child health services and drawing on the work of other inspectorates such as Her Majesty's Inspectorate of Constabulary, and Her Majesty's Inspectorate of Probation.

5.37 The inspection framework would cover the quality of provision, training of staff, outcomes achieved, management capacity, accountability arrangements and the value for money of services overall. Services would be assessed on how well they worked together to meet overall objectives for children, as well as on how well they met their own objectives.

5.38 Inspections would lead to a published report which would assess and give a rating for the quality of provision overall, as well as service by service, and also the quality of joint working such as information sharing and multi-disciplinary teams. The report would be sent to those responsible for all the services involved in the area, and (in respect of local authority services) feed into the Comprehensive Performance Assessment (CPA). The Government will discuss with the Audit Commission and others how best to ensure that these new arrangements are reflected in the revisions to the CPA due in 2005. We would welcome views on the best way to achieve effective integrated inspection of this sort.

5.39 We would expect the Director of Children's Services to take the lead in drawing together a combined action plan in response to the inspection, which would be a useful basis from which to create or extend a Trust to improve the standards and co-ordination of services.

5.40 An integrated inspection framework would be a powerful force to secure genuine integration of local authority services under the new Director of Children's Services, and to encourage a quicker move to Trusts bringing together health and other services. The integrated framework would build upon the child-focused approach developed in joint inspections by tracking children's journeys through the system, and asking them for their views. It could also encourage the involvement of young people in inspection teams.

5.41 As well as inspecting services and assessing management capacity, the integrated inspections could help in the assessment of plans for change drawn up as part of the move to reform service delivery. This would need to be handled carefully so as not to compromise their ability to report objectively on the implementation of the plans.

5.42 A new way of inspecting children's services at local authority level would need to be matched by further integration and reform of inspection and regulation that has a real impact on those who are delivering integrated services at neighbourhood and individual level. For example, residential schools and the new Children's Centres are subject to a number of different registration and inspection arrangements because of the range of services they deliver. The inspectorates responsible already co-operate closely to minimise the burden of inspection, but we will review the formal requirements in order to streamline the inspection process further and enable services to receive a full overall assessment of quality.

Support for improvement

5.43 Given the complexities of the task of developing Children's Trusts, there will be a need to give support to all authorities. The Government is establishing a network of pathfinder authorities to enable them to share developmental expertise. Central Government will also co-ordinate the identification of expertise that sites may need to draw on. The Government will enable authorities to provide support to one another as they identify specialist expertise that they can offer.

5.44 The Government is committed to allowing local flexibility over how national standards are delivered. However, in areas where standards are not being met, it will be essential to have an effective intervention regime in place. Government can also play a role in supporting change through sharing effective practice across the country. The intervention process will need to be transparent and based on the evidence of performance management and inspection. It will operate to build local capacity and will give localities the opportunity to correct problems for themselves where possible.

5.45 We will explore how the principle of earned autonomy can be applied further to children's services and welcomes views on how success could be rewarded, for example through less frequent inspections.

5.46 Where Ministers decide intervention is appropriate, we will require local changes. Options will include:

- allowing one local agency to take over running services currently delivered by another (for example an excellent local authority could take on delivery of key health services for children or vice versa)

- replacing the management of services within a Children's Trust and requiring improvements in co-ordination. Functions could be carried out by another public organisation or under contract with a private or not for profit organisation

- requiring that a service or group of services be exposed to competition, using the Best Value reviewing process

- requiring that the commissioning function is taken on by another organisation

- directing that particular budgets should be pooled

- incentivising authorities to set up trading companies to take on commissioning or provision in failing areas.

Involving children in developing services

5.47 The creation of an organisation defined by its client group rather than professional functions offers an important opportunity to involve children and young people in decision making. This is important in its own right, but also as a way of creating bottom-up pressure for change in services. There are many good examples of local work in this area, particularly through Quality Protects and Connexions Partnerships. These include young people's representation on local scrutiny committees and interview panels for staff, and 'Question Time' events for members and senior officers with young people. We need to spread existing good practice nationally, particularly in terms of engaging hard to reach groups. Views are invited on whether the Government should establish minimum standards for the involvement of children and young people and what they could include.

5.48 The Government is committed to providing more opportunities for children and young people to get involved in the planning, delivery and evaluation of policies and services relevant to them. Young people have been involved in the production of a version of this Green Paper specifically aimed at 11-16 year olds.

5.49 The Government has also involved children and young people to develop:

- national advocacy standards. A children's version of the standards will be published shortly

- standards for children in hospital as part of the development of the NSF for children and in the establishment of patient forums

- the Connexions Service, including scrutinising Connexions Partnerships' business plans and the recruitment of Personal Advisers and Chief Executives

- a Children and Young People's Advisory Forum, involving 26 young people aged 11-17 from a range of backgrounds to advise Government itself on the development of policy.

5.50 To ensure children's and young people's voices are effectively heard, the Government intends to legislate at the earliest opportunity for the appointment of a statutory **Children's Commissioner**. The Commissioner would act as a children's champion independent of Government, and would speak for all children but especially the disadvantaged whose voices are too often drowned out. The Commissioner would advise Government and also engage with others, such as business and the media, whose decisions and actions affect children's lives.

5.51 The Commissioner would develop effective ways to draw on children's views, locally and nationally, and make sure they were fed into policy making. The Commissioner would test the success of policies in terms of what children think and experience. It is essential that the Commissioner does not become dominated by responding to numerous individual complaints and retains its strategic focus.

Its role will be to work with the relevant Ombudsman and statutory bodies to ensure children have quick and easy access to complaints procedures that work. The Commissioner would only investigate individual cases where the issues have a wider relevance to other children, as directed by the Secretary of State.

5.52 To ensure independence, the Commissioner would have the duty to report to Parliament through the Secretary of State for Education and Skills. The Commissioner would report on progress against the outcomes for children, as a result of action by Government and others, drawing on but going wider than the reports arising from joint inspections of children's services.

Next steps

5.53 The Government is keen to ensure the barriers to integration are removed and to put in place some minimum standards in terms of accountability and joining up. We therefore intend to legislate at the earliest opportunity in relation to the above proposals.

5.54 Legislation may also be needed to remove the barriers to Children's Trusts. This will be based on the early feedback from the pathfinders and consultation. Early priorities include further consideration of the current framework for pooling budgets between the NHS and local authorities. Legislation will also be needed to establish inspection arrangements. We will review the adequacy of current powers to intervene in areas falling below national standards.

5.55 The Government seeks views on how it can work with authorities to move forward rapidly on this agenda and support local areas to take on Children's Trust status over a period up to 2006. The intention is to use the local preventative strategies as the basis for a self-audit of children's services in relation to the tests of success set out in this Green Paper and developing local change programmes based on these self-assessments.

5.56 In response to the consultation, the Government will publish an action plan outlining the timetable for change.
In summary this will cover:

● supporting the development of change programmes

● developing and improving support and intervention arrangements

● developing guidance to remove further barriers to pooling and delegation of functions

● improving and rationalising funding, performance indicators, standards, partnership and planning requirements

5.57 The aim of these reforms is to organise services around the needs of children and young people. Achieving this is a shared responsibility between national, regional and local government, partners in the voluntary, community and private sectors and children, young people and families. The Government would like your views on the overall vision, and the role of each partner in making it a reality.

Consultation Questions

Views are invited on all the proposals in this Chapter. In particular:

● How can we encourage better integration of funding for support services for children and young people?

● Should all authorities and other relevant local agencies have a duty to promote the wellbeing of children?

● How best can young people be involved in local decision-making and should the Government establish, for example, minimum standards for this?

● Should Local Safeguarding Children Boards be statutory, and what should their powers and duties be?

● How can we develop, enhance and encourage the Children's Trust model?

● What services should be required to form part of Children's Trusts, and what are the risks in involving more services – for instance, aligning Connexions geographical structures with Children's Trusts?

● How can inspections be integrated better?

Workforce Reform

The Government's proposals build on the lessons from recent workforce reforms in schools, social care, health and the police. Over time, the Government would like to develop a pay and workforce strategy to address recruitment and retention within the children's workforce, and improve its skills and effectiveness. We will achieve this through:

- a workforce reform strategy to improve the skills and effectiveness of the children's workforce and make working with children a more attractive career option. This will review rewards, incentives and relativities across children's practice

- a high profile recruitment campaign

- a comprehensive workload survey

- more flexible and attractive training routes into social work, including expanding work based training routes for graduates

- common occupational standards across children's practice linked to modular qualifications which allow workers to move between jobs more easily

- a common core of training for those who work solely with children and families and those who have wider roles (such as GPs and the police)

- a review undertaken by the Chief Nursing Officer of the contribution that health visitors and other nurses and midwives can make for children at risk

- a leadership development programme to foster high calibre leadership.

A Children's Workforce Unit, based in the Department for Education and Skills, will develop the pay and workforce strategy for those who work with children. The Unit will work with the relevant employers, staff and Government Departments to establish a Sector Skills Council (SSC) for Children and Young People's Services to deliver key parts of the strategy.

6

Challenges

6.1 The Government recognises the tireless efforts of all those working with children. Many frontline staff work under pressure, in challenging circumstances. They possess a wealth and diversity of skills and expertise yet often go without proper appreciation by society for the vital job they do.

6.2 More than four million people in England work with children, or support those working with children. This includes 2.4 million paid staff and 1.8 million unpaid staff and volunteers. In addition, many professionals such as GPs and hospital staff play an important role in supporting children and families, but also have wider responsibilities.

6.3 The box below gives estimates of the numbers of full-time equivalent staff in some of the key roles working with children, young people and their families and employed by local authorities, schools, the NHS, and the private and voluntary sectors.

6.4 The children's workforce is diverse, with people entering at various stages in their lives. However, there is considerable scope for encouraging more people from black and minority ethnic groups, more men and more people with disabilities to enter the children's workforce.

6.5 The new structures and ways of working set out earlier in the Green Paper will help the children's workforce to work more effectively and to join up across professional

Health: 13,000 health visitors, 2,500 school nurses, almost 6,000 speech and language therapists, and over 50,000 other health professionals including paediatricians, children's nurses and midwives

Early years and childcare: 83,000 early years workers and 280,000 childcare workers

Schools workforce: 440,000 teachers and 230,000 school support staff

Social workers: 40,000 children and families social workers

Education welfare: 3,000 education welfare officers

Connexions: 7,000 Connexions personal advisers

Youth work: 7,000 youth workers

Play: 30,000 play workers

Sport: 400,000 sports and leisure workers

Youth offending: 5,000 people working in Youth Offending Teams and 5,000 people working in the juvenile secure estate

boundaries. But they will not be enough in themselves to tackle some current issues. This Chapter sets out how the Government will address two key challenges: raising the attractiveness of working with children in order to improve recruitment and retention; and improving the skills and effectiveness of the workforce.

Recruitment and retention

6.6 Recruitment and retention problems are not uniform and there are variations between different job roles and in different parts of the country. There are significant problems of recruitment and retention in social work where the national vacancy rate is 11 percent. There is also an estimated national shortage of 8,000 foster carers.

6.7 Figure 1 below shows the stark comparisons between vacancy rates across different public sector professions, and between rates in London and the rest of the country.

6.8 Problems with recruitment and retention have a number of causes:

● image and status. Social workers have suffered from a poor public image, and childcare is often seen as low status

● variable management and supervision. This is a problem across the public sector which is identified in the Audit Commission's *Recruitment and Retention* report (2002), and re-emphasised in Lord Laming's report

● workload and bureaucracy. High vacancy rates contribute to pressure on those in post, and requirements designed to secure accountability impose increasing demands for information. As a result, some social workers spend less than 30 percent of their time working directly with children and families, performing tasks that might be better done by others

Figure 1: Public sector vacancy rates

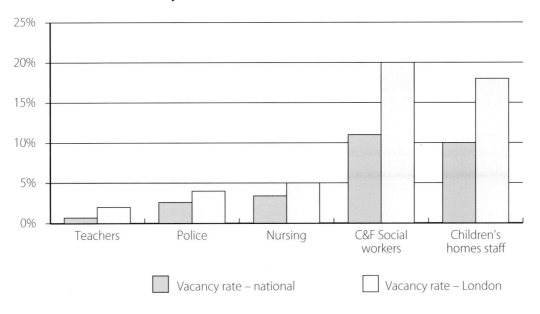

Legend: Vacancy rate – national ◻ Vacancy rate – London

- expansion. New initiatives and increasing investment run the risk of competing for a limited pool of staff

- complex pay issues which may play a part in recruitment and retention difficulties in some areas, and need further exploration. For many groups including social workers, available flexibilities may not have been enough to ensure employers attract the workforce they require.

Skills, teamwork and flexibility

6.9 Knowledge and understanding of child protection procedures among frontline staff who work with children is often patchy and underdeveloped. There is often little initial training and support for staff working in children's homes and limited routes towards attaining qualifications. Currently, only 27 percent of non-managerial staff in children's homes hold a relevant professional qualification, including the five percent who are qualified social workers.

6.10 A number of those currently working with children have roles which overlap in some important respects. For example an education welfare officer, a Connexions personal adviser or a learning mentor may all play the key worker role with a child who truants from school. But current training, as well as pay and conditions, are very different for each role. These roles also have close professional competence links with frontline social workers.

6.11 Within the more integrated structures and working practices set out in earlier

Chapters, it will remain the case that some children and families need support from a range of professionals. We need to establish new cultures in the workplace so that individual professionals work horizontally across professional boundaries rather than vertically in professional hierarchies.

6.12 Everyone working with children needs to be trained to do their own job well. They also need to know how their role fits with that of others. They need the skills to work positively with, and draw on the expertise of, other professionals and support staff. Among other things this will avoid unnecessary and unproductive referrals. This is true not only for those working with children with identified needs, but also for teachers and GPs who can be the first to spot emerging problems.

Progress so far

6.13 The Government has recognised the central importance of the children's workforce to the delivery of improved services, and the need for pay and workforce strategies to underpin reforms. Individual departments have taken significant steps to improve training for those working with children.

6.14 Alongside increased teacher recruitment, a major transformation of the school workforce is underway, with the development of new and more flexible roles for support staff in schools, including pastoral care, behaviour management, and counselling. The proposals in this Chapter will complement school workforce reform and support the implementation of *Raising standards and tackling workload: a national agreement.*

6.15 In the case of the social care workforce, reforms include:

- a new three year social work degree, to begin this year, designed to increase the competence to practise of those completing social work training, to raise the professional status of the occupation, and to bring it more in line with national and international peers

- a new post-qualifying childcare award for social workers

- the General Social Care Council (GSCC) is beginning to register the social work profession

- the Social Care Institute of Excellence (SCIE) is collecting and spreading good practice

- changing workforce programme pilots – the first five of which will be up and running this year – will support the reform of the social care workforce by rigorously testing new workforce roles against their ability to meet the needs of users

- the social care workforce development grants to social care employers are being trebled from £/2 million in 2002-03 to £226 million by 2005-06

6.16 Following the Victoria Climbié Inquiry, the Government commissioned a review of training in inter-agency work and communication in child protection services.

The review is led by the General Social Care Council, and involves all the professional bodies responsible for training professional staff from agencies engaged in child protection work – the police, social services, education and the NHS. It is due to report in autumn 2003.

6.17 More flexible entry routes into the children's professions are being developed for non-graduates:

- the Youth Justice Board has developed a new qualifications framework and new learning and development programmes for youth justice staff and is piloting Advanced Modern Apprenticeships

- the employment-based Graduate Teacher Programme (GTP) and the Registered Teacher Programme (RTP) involve trainees being employed by a school as an unqualified teacher while they follow an individual training programme

- there are a growing number of employment based routes into social work. The Department of Health this year introduced a Trainee Social Worker Programme that will fund the equivalent of 600 posts.

6.18 Connexions has developed multi-agency training for professionals working with 13-19 year olds. Staff from a range of backgrounds – careers, social work, education welfare, the voluntary sector – learn together to develop a shared understanding of how to work across agencies to improve outcomes for young people. To date, over 7,500 people have participated in Connexions training.

Way forward

6.19 Our aim is to ensure that all children's services have enough people, of a high calibre and with the right skills to meet the needs of children and families. All Government Departments are now developing pay and workforce strategies following the cross cutting review of the public sector labour market. In line with this approach, we will develop a pay and workforce strategy to improve the skills and effectiveness of the children's workforce. It will be based on a thorough assessment of the roles, skills, supply and demand and trends for all parts of the children's workforce and plans for change in service delivery.

6.20 The reform agenda will be driven forward though a new Children's Workforce Unit in DfES. The Unit will be complemented by a new Sector Skills Council (SSC) for Children and Young People's Services to ensure that employers are fully involved in the process of reform.

6.21 The reform of the children's workforce is aimed at:

- raising the attractiveness and status of the work
- improving skills and collaborative working.

Raising the attractiveness of the work

6.22 An early priority must be to develop a better understanding of the demand for people to work with children in current roles, and the skills which are required in each. Mapping demand against current trends in training and recruitment should provide an understanding of the cause of any shortfalls and how to bridge the gap. Another early priority will be to define the precise range of roles and occupations on which reforms will focus.

6.23 Following this detailed analysis, the Government plans to develop a package of measures, broadly similar to those already in place for teaching, to increase recruitment and retention for others working with children. Views are invited on the following package of measures, which is based on what the current workforce – frontline staff and their managers – say would make a real difference.

6.24 In mapping the current workforce and planning new developments it will be important to build upon and support the role of the many volunteers who devote their time and skills to helping children and families. Some volunteers will welcome the opportunity to move into the paid workforce, if training and work patterns can be adjusted to fit their needs. Most will want to remain in an unpaid role, but might welcome opportunities for training and development jointly with those in linked services. All professionals need to understand the important roles which volunteers play, offering readily accessible support that is rooted in the local community.

Pay and financial incentives

6.25 The Children's Workforce Unit will work with employers and staff to develop a workforce reform strategy to improve the skills and effectiveness of the children's workforce. This will review rewards, incentives and relativities across children's practice with the aim of moving towards a career framework that fairly rewards skills and responsibilities, and ensures effective incentives for good practitioners to stay on the front line.

6.26 The Unit will consider how to resolve recruitment and retention problems in different regional and local labour markets, and in particular areas of children's practice such as social work. Progress will depend on reform which delivers better outcomes for children and on resources.

6.27 There are currently many different arrangements for determining pay and conditions for staff who work with children, including Pay Review Bodies for teachers, health service staff and others. These should

---

Health Service: Agenda for Change

Under the Agenda for Change agreement, staff will be placed in one of eight pay bands on the basis of their knowledge, responsibility, skills and the effort needed for the job, rather than on the basis of their current job title.

NHS productivity should be improved both by the focus on a better skilled workforce working in new ways, and by breaking down barriers between different roles with nurses doing some of the task traditionally reserved for doctors, and support staff taking on some of the nurses' tasks.

School Workforce Reform

Advanced Skills Teachers (ASTs) posts have created a new career path for excellent teachers who want to continue as teachers and use their skills to support the professional development of their colleagues. Over the last year AST numbers have expanded from just under 1,000 in post in January 2002 to around 3,000 at the end of March 2003.

In January 2003, Ministers signed an historic national agreement with head teacher, teacher and support staff unions and local government employers on the principles and practical implementation of school workforce reform. It has paved the way for changes to the teachers' contract; more support staff in extended roles, including personal assistants for teachers, cover supervisors and higher level teaching assistants; and a concerted attack on bureaucracy, including the establishment of a new Implementation Review Unit, featuring a panel of serving practitioners.

continue their important work. The Children's Workforce Unit will explore with stakeholders how to support employers on issues such as roles, skills, recruitment and reward for people who work with children across the labour market as a whole, taking account of regional and local differences. That does not mean moving away from trusted systems for setting pay for particular groups.

6.28 The Children's Workforce Unit will need to consider the following questions in developing reforms:

- what should be the precise scope and focus of its reforms?

- what could be achieved through new pay arrangements, and what are the risks of change?

- how can resources be targeted at areas with the greatest recruitment and retention challenges?

- how best can fairness as well as efficiency be ensured within such a system?

- what use should be made of golden hellos and training bursaries?

- how can good performance be incentivised and rewarded?

- is there potential to develop a scheme to support the retention of vital frontline social care staff, drawing on the lessons from the Advanced Skills Teachers initiative?

- how can flexible working patterns be supported?

- how can the 'climbing frame' qualifications approach developed in the early years sector whereby people can move across different professions as well as progress upwards be applied more broadly?

Bureaucracy and workload

6.29 The Children's Workforce Unit will undertake a comprehensive workload survey to look at how to increase the time spent working with children and families, by cutting out unnecessary paperwork, improving support from supervisors and administrators, and better use of ICT.

Recruitment and entry routes

6.30 The Children's Workforce Unit will develop a high profile recruitment campaign for entry into the children's workforce, including general advertising and targeted recruitment. It will examine how to support people with no or few traditional education qualifications to enter the profession through modern apprenticeships and foundation degrees. Building on the lessons from the Graduate Teacher Programme, it will also examine how to extend flexible work based entry routes for graduates.

6.31 It will also consider how to support people who are changing jobs mid-life and women returning to the labour market after having children. Flexible and high quality routes into working with children will help to increase both the quantity and quality of recruits. Good professional development for frontline staff, and for their leaders and managers, can also have an important effect on morale and retention.

6.32 The Children's Workforce Unit will also examine how Jobcentre Plus can:

- promote careers in working with children, young people and families

- explore the development of its role in commissioning childcare training, given the important influence this can have in helping people into work

- work actively with the voluntary sector and community groups to match people with opportunities to work with children in their local community.

Improving skills and teamwork

Working together

6.33 The Government is committed to working with children's workers to deliver world class services. To that end, the Children's Workforce Unit will examine how to develop collaborative approaches with frontline staff to identify and overcome the barriers they face in improving services to children. This sort of approach has delivered significant improvements in the NHS.

Evolving roles

6.34 While their roles are distinct, there are already some common elements across 'children's practice' in the work of education welfare officers, learning mentors and Connexions personal advisers, support staff for those with special educational needs, youth workers, YOT staff, and children's social workers. Occupational mapping of the first three roles is already in hand. As the new approaches set out in this Green Paper are developed, those elements in common will

become clearer, as will the distinctive part that those playing each role should be able to contribute. As joint working becomes the norm, clarity about roles and responsibilities will be all the more important. This may mean that some of the labels worn today will need to be changed in order to communicate clearly who is doing what within a reconfigured, modernised workforce.

6.35 Around half of local authorities have career grade progression schemes in place for social work staff. The Government would like to see an extension of this recognition of advanced skills in the workforce so that the most skilled professional staff can be rewarded and newly qualified staff given strong incentives to develop their expertise. Developments could involve:

- an extension of the current senior practitioner posts, linked to a role in disseminating good practice outside their immediate workplace, based on the lessons of Advanced Skills Teachers

- consideration of a consultant social worker role at a very high level of practitioner seniority as already developed by a small number of local authorities.

Leadership

6.36 The reforms set out in Chapter Five are aimed at clarifying accountability, and creating greater space for leadership by placing key services under the control of Directors of Children's Services. The quality of leadership will be critical as children's services go through a period of reform and culture change.

6.37 To support this, the Children's Workforce Unit will develop a programme to foster the highest calibre of leadership in children's services, building on the work done by existing employers and departments. The Unit will also have an important role in supporting the efforts of local authorities in recruiting and developing Directors of Children's Services.

Common core training and continuing professional development

6.38 The Government intends to develop national occupational standards and a modular training and qualifications structure across the widest possible range of workers in children's services. This will enable all people working with children to share a common core of skills, knowledge and competence and help people move across professional boundaries. The Children's Workforce Unit will also seek to increase the availability of high quality continuous professional development for all who work with children.

6.39 A common core of standards and training will support the development of more effective integrated services across professional disciplines, and promote more flexible career progression and development. Clearer recognition of roles and skills will be relevant in reviewing pay issues: both ensuring there are incentives to develop and use new skills, and considering whether there are barriers to career development.

6.40 Those working in more specialised professional roles, such as GPs, teachers and police and prison officers, need a common language and understanding of children's needs, as the basis for positive professional relationships.

6.41 The Children's and Young People's Unit commissioned the Interdisciplinary Childhood and Youth Studies Network to propose the content for a common core of training for all professionals working with children. They suggested content organised under six headings:

Nottingham – Joint Training and Learning

Nottingham has developed an innovative approach through a consultation forum bringing together social work practitioners and colleagues from other disciplines including the statutory and voluntary sector.

Additional expertise can be called on for specific issues, for example, domestic violence, mental health, drugs and alcohol.

The consultation forum allows practitioners to reflect on particular cases where there are complex issues around safeguarding children; to learn from other disciplines; and to take that learning back into their workplace, as well as identifying ways forward for individual children.

- understanding the developmental nature of childhood

- parents, parenting and family life

- managing transitions

- understanding child protection

- understanding risk and protective factors

- listening to and involving children and young people.

6.42 We would welcome views on whether these headings are broadly right and how we might best ensure that training for different professional groups develops a shared understanding of the relevant issues. There may be particular advantage in delivering such training to multi-disciplinary groups of workers or of students.

Health visitors, children's nursing and midwifery
6.43 Health visitors are responsible for assessing and responding to the health needs of children, families and communities. The workforce has an important role in supporting children and families in the early years as well as a wider role in improving the health of the population as a whole. Increasingly, health visitors are working in multi-disciplinary teams with others such as nursery nurses and community development workers to promote child and family health. There is scope to further develop inter-disciplinary working with some health visitors and other nurses working in integrated children and families teams alongside other health, education and social care professionals. This should help to deliver more accessible, joined up services with optimum use of diverse skills.

6.44 The Chief Nursing Officer will undertake a review of the contribution that health visitors and other nurses and midwives can make to children at risk in the light of the Green Paper and their wider public health and health care responsibilities.

Child and Adolescent Mental Health Services (CAMHS)
6.45 Delivering improved child mental health depends upon enlarging the capacity of the child and adolescent mental health workforce. Children's mental health is the business of all the people, agencies and services in contact with children and young people. Everyone with significant professional contact with children and young people should be able to recognise and deal with normal developmental problems and know when to ask for assistance with more complex problems. To achieve this they need proper skills and training.

6.46 The Government will develop a coherent multi-agency strategy for mental health skill development within all children's agencies. This will build on the initiatives currently underway, including the development of mental health awareness training for Youth Offending Teams and guidance to school staff on their role and how to seek further specialist help. It will also address the continuing and additional training needs of the CAMHS workforce, including from all those agencies that make up a comprehensive CAMHS service, and the development of new career pathways.

Delivery

6.47 Encouraging more people to work with children and enhancing the skills of those who work with children is a priority. It requires considerable work by employers, the Government and statutory agencies to deliver reform in this diverse sector. We need quickly to identify and address workforce development priorities. And the voluntary sector will be an important partner in these discussions.

6.48 Key steps to be taken include:

- an assessment of present and future demand and need

- a clear and accurate assessment of employment patterns and the skills required for work in this sector

- an assessment of skills supply and demand, considering issues of recruitment and retention in different regional and local labour markets, workforce turnover, pay, skills gaps and shortages and how human resource policies affect these

- the development of a strategy for skills in this sector, encompassing a modular training programme, and with clear links to the skills strategy for the voluntary and community services sector that will be published in the autumn

- the development of a targeted recruitment campaign, specifically designed for this sector

- a review of occupational standards and skills development provision, the identification of significant gaps and action to fill these

- commissioning high quality training provision where the market is currently not providing this, and stimulating innovation in delivery to ensure maximum access by people working or preparing to work in the sector

- work with employers and staff to consider how a new approach to pay could address current problems and support desired changes.

6.49 The Children's Workforce Unit will co-ordinate work between key partners to deliver these functions and produce a pay and workforce strategy for the children's workforce. The initial phase of work will be completed by spring 2004, in order to feed into the next Spending Review. The new Unit will work closely alongside the existing School Workforce Unit in DfES. It will bring together employers, Government Departments, statutory bodies, the voluntary sector and other relevant agencies to deliver this work. These partners include employer-led Sector Skills Councils with responsibility for employers working with children; Employers' Organisation for Local Government; General Social Care Council; other relevant employer groups and associations; bodies responsible for funding and commissioning training and its inspection, including the Higher Education Funding Council (England), Learning and

Skills Council, Adult Learning Inspectorate, Commission for Social Care Inspection, Ofsted, and Government Departments.

6.50 Strong employer leadership for this diverse sector is essential. The Children's Workforce Unit will work with all the relevant key partners to establish a Sector Skills Council (SSC) for Children and Young People's Services. We would envisage the Council assuming responsibility for the widest possible range of functions listed above. As SSCs are UK-wide bodies, the Council would need to be sufficiently flexible to address both the common and differing skill needs of people who work with children in England, Scotland, Wales and Northern Ireland.

6.51 The development of a Sector Skills Council will take time, and the Government will need to take an initial lead. We intend to prioritise work on children's social work and related professions, but a Children and Young People's Services SSC will also need to cover the wider children's workforce, from early years right through to Connexions and youth work. One key role would be to encourage new models of high quality training, as responsive as possible to the employer and customer rather than institutional priorities. This might in due course be secured by direct funding of professional courses, as the Teacher Training Agency funds initial teacher training. Improved training could also be supported by integrated inspections for professional training, building on the proposed

integrated inspection framework described in Chapter Five.

6.52 Taking forward this demanding reform agenda will require close partnership working with a range of existing bodies such as the TTA and the GSCC. Good relationships will need to be established with the wide range of employers who have an interest in this work, and whose engagement will be essential to the success of any strategy. Many of the employers in the sector are small and it will be important to ensure they are able to take part in, influence and benefit from discussions. The Sector Skills Development Agency and the Small Business Service have an important role to play here.

6.53 Local authorities and the Children's Trusts within them will remain the major employers of those on whom the initial work of the Unit will focus. The close involvement of the Local Government Association and the Office of the Deputy Prime Minister will be essential to their success. The workforce reforms will be given an added impetus not only by the changes to structures and working practices described earlier, but also by the streamlined regime of standard setting and inspection which will show how the skills and knowledge of the workforce contribute to improved outcomes for children.

Consultation Questions

The Government would welcome views on the proposals set out in this Chapter. In particular:

- What are the priorities that the workforce reform strategy should tackle to improve recruitment, retention and incentives for those working with children?

- Should all those working with children share a common core of skills and knowledge?

- Should there be a common qualifications structure for all those in key roles working with children? If so, which roles should it cover?

The Consultation Process and Summary of Questions

Thank you for taking the time to respond to the questions set out below on this Green Paper, *Every Child Matters*.

We welcome any further comments you may have on this Green Paper or on the Regulatory Impact Assessment of it which can be accessed online at www.dfes.gov.uk/everychildmatters

To take part in the consultation, response forms can be downloaded at the above web address.

Completed questionnaires and other responses, should be sent to the address shown below by **1 December 2003**.

By post: **Children's Green Paper, Consultation Unit, Level 1, Area B, Castle View House, East Lane, Runcorn, WA7 2GJ.**

By e-mail: **Consultation1.CHILDRENSGP@dfes.gsi. gov.uk**

Consultation Questions

Chapter 2

Views are invited on the proposals set out in this Chapter. In particular:

● How can we improve support for unaccompanied asylum-seeking children, building on the work of the Children's Panel?

● How can we ensure that serious welfare concerns are appropriately dealt with alongside criminal proceedings?

● How can we encourage clusters of schools to work together around extended schools?

Chapter 3

Views are invited on the proposals set out in this Chapter. In particular:

● How can good quality decision-making by social services in relation to achieving permanence for the children for whom they are responsible best be achieved?

- Building on Choice Protects, what more can we do to recruit and retain more foster carers who are able to meet the needs of looked after children?

- How can local authorities, working with the voluntary, community and private sectors, develop a range of specialist parenting support services?

- Working with local authorities and other existing providers what steps should the Government take to make home visiting services more widely available?

- What further action could be taken to extend the use of direct payments by families with disabled children?

- What more could be done to improve services for children and families of offenders?

Chapter 4

Views are invited on the proposals set out in this Chapter. In particular:

- What currently gets in the way of information sharing, and how can we remove the barriers?

- What should be the thresholds and triggers for sharing information about a child?

- What are the circumstances (in addition to child protection and youth offending) under which information about a child could or must be shared without the consent of the child or their carers?

- Should information on parents and carers, such as domestic violence, imprisonment, mental health or drug problems, be shared?

- How can we ensure that no children slip through the system?

- What issues might stand in the way of effective information transfer across local authority boundaries?

- Should a unique identifying number be used?

- Views are also invited in the proposals relating to multi-disciplinary teams:

    – What are the barriers to developing them further in a range of settings?

    – How can we ensure multi-disciplinary teams have greater leverage over mainstream and specialist services?

Chapter 5

Views are invited on the proposals set out in this Chapter. In particular:

- How can we encourage better integration of funding for support services for children and young people?

- Should all authorities and other relevant local agencies have a duty to promote the wellbeing of children?

- How best can young people be involved in local decision making and should the Government, for example, establish minimum standards for this?

- Should Children and Young People's Strategic Partnerships and Local

Safeguarding Boards be statutory, and what should their powers and duties be?

- How can we develop, enhance and encourage the Children's Trust model?

- What services should be required to form part of Children's Trusts, and what are the risks involved in involving more services- for instance, aligning Connexions geographical structures with Children's Trusts?

- How can inspections be integrated better?

Chapter 6

Views are invited on the proposals set out in this Chapter. In particular:

- What are the priorities that the workforce reform strategy should tackle to improve recruitment, retention and incentives for those working with children?

- Should all those working with children share a common core of skills and knowledge?

- Should there be a common qualifications structure for all those in key roles working with children? If so, which roles should it cover?

Timetable for Action on Information Sharing

1. By the end of September 2003 local authorities should:

- have mechanisms in place which ensure that IRT supports the delivery of their local preventative strategy[1]

- have a named individual to whom agencies and professionals working with children and young people can pass details of children and young people found to be missing from education. This individual would take the lead in brokering support for such children and young people through the most appropriate agencies

- have evidence of engagement with all children's services (statutory and voluntary) in the development of IRT

- ensure all staff involved in delivering services to children understand the role and responsibilities of Data Protection Officers in relation to IRT

- audit of current practice including the identification of information-sharing protocols, assessment processes, strategies for securing the engagement of stakeholders and mechanisms for ensuring that children in need of support receive appropriate services at the earliest opportunity. The audit should cover arrangements within the local authority, between the local authority and other statutory agencies and between the local authority and voluntary sector agencies.

- ensure that all agencies understand the legal framework that enables them to share information.

---

1 Local preventative strategies (LPS) seek to co-ordinate the effective planning, commissioning and delivery of preventative services to children and young people within each local authority.

2. By the end of March 2004 local authorities should:

- be able to demonstrate that more effective information sharing between health, education and social care is improving services for children who display one or more risk factors

- ensure that practitioners working with children have a shared understanding of assessment, risk factors, service thresholds that trigger action and service eligibility criteria

- have a service directory providing comprehensive information on local providers, eligibility criteria, geographical location and referral procedures

- have procedures for keeping this service directory up to date and for ensuring professionals working with children and young people have access – allowing public access where possible

- publish a privacy statement to inform children, young people and their families about confidentiality and access to records

- have protocols in place for information sharing covering health services, education services and social care; and in development for all other agencies providing services to children and young people, including the police and Youth Offending Teams

- publish guidance on obtaining and documenting consent (including information leaflets for children, young people and their families, and consent forms)

- understand the authority's specific business needs in relation to information sharing

- have considered practical links between systems at a local level, with agreed standards for data collection, storage, retrieval and transfer, based on the e-Government Interoperability Framework (e-GIF).

Printed in the UK by The Stationery Office Limited
on behalf of the Controller of Her Majesty's Stationery Office
Id 153606   09/03